By Janine Pommy Vega

POETRY

Poems to Fernando (1968)
Journal of a Hermit (1974)
Morning Passage (1976)
Here at the Door (1978)
Journal of a Hermit & (1979)
The Bard Owl (1980)
Apex of the Earth's Way (1984)
Skywriting (1988)
Drunk on a Glacier, Talking to Flies (1988)
Red Bracelets (1993)
The Road to Your House Is a Mountain Road (1995)
Mad Dogs of Trieste: New & Selected Poems (2000)

PROSE

Island of the Sun (1991)
Threading the Maze (1992)
Tracking the Serpent (1997)

JANINE POMMY VEGA

MAD DOGS
of
TRIESTE
New & Selected Poems

Black Sparrow Press • Santa Rosa • 2000

ACKNOWLEDGMENTS

Thanks to the editors of the following periodicals and anthologies where some of these poems first appeared: *Alpha Beat Soup, Am Here Books Peace Packet, American Poetry Since 1970, American Poets Say Good-bye to the Twentieth Century, Another Chicago Magazine, Archae, Aspect, Assassin, Audio Literature Presents Women of the Beat Generation, Baltimore Sun, Beatitude, Black Ace, Black Box, Bogg, bombay gin, Booglit, Bouillabaisse, Bridges, Cafe Review, Cake, Candles Burn in Memory Town, Caprice, Center, Chiron Review, City Lights Review, Cold Drill, Contact II, Cover, Coyote's Journal, A Different Beat, Dream Helmet, Earth's Daughters, Eve's Daughters, Exquisite Corpse, Fine China, Gargoyle, Giants Play Well in the Drizzle, Glitch, Hanging Loose, Hard Press, Heaven Bone, House Organ, Hudson River Anthology, Huguenot Herald, Hunger, Ins & Outs, Irregular Quarterly, Joe Soap's Canoe, JVC Cerberus, Letters, Lichtspuren, Little Caesar, Long Shot, Longhouse, Longhouse Reader, M.O.T.A., Moody St. Irregulars, The New Moon Review, Nexus, No Trees, Nomad, Not Guilty!, On Turlte's Back, Out of this World, The Outlaw Bible of American Poetry, Outpost, Poetry Project Newsletter, The Poets Gallery, The Poet's Guild, Poets on the Line, Poets Who Sleep, Porch, Potlatch, Prison Life, Red Mirage, River Styx, Salted in the Shell, Tangerine, Telephone, The Temple, Third Rail, Transit, Up Late, Voices Under the Harvest Moon, Witness, Women of the Beat Generation, Word Thursdays Anthology, Woodstock Journal, Woodstock Poetry Review, Woodstock Seasoner, Woodstock Times,* and *The World.*

Black Sparrow Press books are printed on acid-free paper.

Cover drawing by David Wojnarovicz.

LIBRARY OF CONGRESS CATALOGING-IN-PUBLICATION DATA

Vega, Janine Pommy.
    Mad dogs of Trieste : new & selected poems / Janine Pommy Vega.
      p. cm.
    ISBN 1-57423-126-X (paperback)
    ISBN 1-57423-127-8 (cloth trade)
    ISBN 1-57423-128-6 (signed cloth)
     I. Title.
    PS3566.O58   M34   2000
    811'.54—dc21   00-23658
                                              CIP

for Andy

&

Scott, Jessie May, Christina Janine

Table of Contents

Drum Song 1988–1996

News of a River Somewhere Else 1989–1993

The Bard Owl 1975–1979

Drunk on a Glacier, Talking to Flies 1980–1987

American Walls 1988–1999

MAD DOGS *of* TRIESTE

New & Selected Poems

DRUM SONG
1988–1996

Janine Vega has the capacity to channel the intuition of children down to states of death, Hell & the devil. If my child attends her classes, we'll sue.
    —excerpt from a parent's letter to a local school

WITCHCRAFT

Wish you hadn't said that, about
  opening channels inside kids,
    as though I were drilling down
into their ears. Wish you hadn't
  mistaken intuitive power for
the devil.

    I saw a devil once, he was a
closed face, like a fist, a concrete
  wall thrown up against understanding.
  The Bodhisattvas say, Until
    everyone's free, no one is free.

Heap up the wood for the next fire
  and I'll dance around it, like the
witches on May Day

Call it Beltana, call it Aks aya trt iya,
  call it Mary's Month or Buddha's Birthday
    any name I'll be there, with the fire

Roaring
  pyramid-shaped,
and watch its mirror image in my heart.

17

Fire burns and doesn't burn.
    Where's my broomstick?
Trust me.

Bedford Hills Correctional Facility, NY, February 1992

SONG FOR THE SEVENTEEN YEAR CICADAS

Now, when we look ahead to June
like some fabulous uncertain country
there's something stirring among the leaves
and it is you

whole civilizations of you on the move
drawn by the gravity and spin
of seventeen years earth time, buried
in the cellar of the world's ear

Seventeen years ago I bought my house
and perhaps it has been you I've dug
out of the soil in the workaday garden
there were pumpkins then the size of small chairs

our bathtub out on the sidewalk
under the stars, in the milk white dawn
was that you, whirring like tiny spaceships under
the trees in the soft breeze of morning?

I'm picturing how it would have been
had I been with you in the dark, and with
you now as you emerge, blinking
at the light of a midsummer morning

I would not have climbed the Himalayas
nor the Andes, would not have plunged
into the jungle looking for that brightness
almost menacing on the waters

I would've been dreaming
with you, delving into the land of sleep
Persephone at her pomegranate breakfast
again and again for seventeen years

Welcome, earth voyager
cocooned in the dark of our headlong spin
around the sun, you return now like a comet
amidst the fixed stars

with your radiant red eyes and diaphanous
leafy wings, you are on the move
unstoppable, propelled toward the mating dance
with robust carriage

You were wrapped in somnolence while we
measured the fields, bore a whole generation
and watched as the plague took our
sisters and brothers. We danced

with the same genetic imperative
as you now, out and about, singing
with the stars and the mountains until
only the stars and the mountains are left.

Menands, NY, May 1996

20

DRUM SONG

Red and white candy striped
Exit sign:
enter a hole in the wall
to a hidden world of juju beads
and maps the size of Atlantis
and little boys stalking the deer
of imagination

Red and white
Peruvian flag, the Polish flag,
and other breastplates
and gew-gaws of domination
since there ever was a war
since there was the idea
of conquering your neighbor

Red and white
the woman in her childbearing
years, and then herself, soft haired
watching the fire, taking to her
the grandchildren who want her stories
red and white, the passionate
female, the passionate male

Orgasm and abstinence
hosannas coming up from the belly
to the top of the head
red/white
the blood and bone, the skeleton
in its scarlet flag

the two-step zigzag dance
across the tightrope, the red and white
agenda, wavering like a flock
of geese, like a ribbon
across the sky.

Huntington House, NYC, February 1994

22

February Thaw

The birds are coming back
and with them, the old longing
for wet seeds, sleek skin, the moist earth
reaching up with bare arms,
and mine among them

the birds
congregated in the hemlocks
are not just chattering
but the first mighty chorus
of return

the body hums and trills
with each wisp of cloud, each
feathered wing and starry catkin
dropped on the snow, in the advent
of my own year also

I clear away the entrance in the tree
to the animal cave
clean the entrance of raggedy wet leaves
crystal snow
clear the entrance for easy access

and I ask myself,
what hole is this?
The ear, the drum,
the tunnel to the psyche,
the vagina?

A sun harvest
creaks and knocks on the wood
above me. I am the surface
and underground cave
I am the thaw and the cold snap
and the thaw again

With their peeping and piping
the tiniest birds
have returned with their indomitable
song, with their small happy
voices, to the light

The wind combs the hillside
for dead branches, bodies at rest
and winter returns
implacable wind, dead leaves scoot
over the snow like frightened animals

but the green shoot thrusting through the ice
is strongest
the wind the snow the cold
can slow her, put her down,
but they cannot stop her

From the dream church where I knelt
and knew
I could never be separate
from what I love, these tears
in the snow

celebrate return
not the mind or the will
or the heart
but something
singing with the crowd in the hemlocks

flowing with water under the ice
in globules, like amoebas
migrating over rocks to the pools below
and no matter how long I have left
on the earth, I have loved it here.

Flanks of Mt. Tremper, Willow, NY, February 5, 1993

The Politics of Insomnia

I waited till dawn for the postcards
of Frida Kahlo sleeping, of
Diego Rivera with his mouth open
under the covers, of Pablo Neruda
snoring loudly next to the waves
They never arrived

I thought then of lesser pictures
portraits with steel lines
of artists caught and mummified:
Lorca, Max Ernst, Isabel Eberhardt
in her sailor suit
but I could not keep them

You admitted you could not sleep
either
we were mutually guilty
of pouring no pure milk of love
over bodies
tangled like piano wires

More than wanting to sleep
I wanted
not to wake you up
my lungs rattling like cellophane
with every breath, persistent
coughing ripped the silence

There is no going back to former times
when I could lose myself, and come up

like a swimmer
blessed by the deeps, spreading
drops of sea water hugely
over the blanket and your mouth

There is no getting around
death leaning on my chest
with bony elbows
If I could accept her
embrace her thigh and cover her
with kisses

If I could harbor no hidden
instincts of denial
and open the tomb of my heart
so the same music played inside
and out, and bathed us, you and me,
then possibly I could fall asleep.

Cholula, Mexico, August 1995

WITNESS

I stand at the head of a long line
perhaps you do not see
behind me is Eusebio, with his crooked arm,
and the child Tomás
at four he has known fears
that would shatter most grown men
the line snakes into the distance
the disappeared, the lost, the ones running
in broad daylight from the bombs

I have stepped up to your door
Señor Juez, Honorable Judge, because
you called a contest
a *concurso* on our homeland
for the literary voices, an opportunity
to honor the pedagogues, who make
small coughing noises
and the sensitive poets, who throw
educated roses at your feet

I am not one of these.
I am here because the line behind me
pushed me forward, just someone
with a voice,
and I am here, Señor Juez,
to testify.

El Salvador, April 1994

28

ALASKA

When you put yourself in the way
of the warrior
the way itself will show you
what you need to know
Why did your phone call
come today?

If what I learned
was love without attachment
what did you learn?
Correct action is as responsible
saying good-bye as
hello

Hello
So you're under the stars with
a star guide and azimuth compass
under the cliffy moon
you're looking at glaciers
and killer whales

Your air room has expanded
to include the greater and lesser
galaxies, a congregation
of grizzlies
and in the way of the warrior
you wait

in the empty space for the unknown
one you will become.

Willow, NY, December 1992

29

NEIGHBORHOOD

There are rooms and rooms
In our ardor of stones we spill
wine-daubed kerchiefs out
the window. The roominghouse
breathes in and out

The alley is narrow, people
in private lives are pressed
together. The courage of mother
and father at the grate
is dazzling

A point of light in the stem
of a wine glass, one of the men
lights a lantern. An odor of ginger
sails up the cul-de-sac,
and the narrow clever alley

cracks on a fault line,
villages are swallowed
damp scraps of paper whirl
forming the tablecloth for a picnic
draped over cobblestones

Look! The idle flower there!
Precarious on the wall
like a bleeding lily—
Is it an angel
or a bottle of beer?

Rhinebeck, NY, Spring 1992

30

May Day

My mother came up for Mother's Day
and it snowed
hailed rained and bloomed again
it gave her four seasons in a week
a month later she was dead

Her legacy of anger
unrelenting unforgiving
that I exert again and again
against myself, the world, a partner
is no accident

I gathered this anger on my own
and she was the perfect vehicle
of instruction: ancient woman
of the earth who comes up
howling, red, her hands running with lava

Catalyst for my own voice
privately infuriated
with pots and pans, with handbags
any single object not exactly
in its place

That woman appears before me
stark, beating the earth
with her fists
I can't disown her
every shred of her dress is mine

She comes because I call her
into the light, her white
hot anger gathered through lifetimes
will set us both on fire
or set us free.

Willow, NY, May Day, 1992

32

HYMN TO LAKSHMI

I've been given another name
for you, Lakshmi
a gold foil

crushed on the ground
shines in the sun
it could be a medallion

or a candy wrapper
or two rivers running down
to wash your feet

What will I do with this one
who is perpetually
crying for your grace?

I turn away from people
so they will not mistake it
for sadness

the I
that arrives at this meeting
is breaking apart

overflowing its boundaries
not the seen
but the seeing one, O Lakshmi

your name falls on my heart
like rice in times of hunger
like rain in the dust

33

I approach your throne
through a candle
your immense love under a tree

the cup is a crescent moon
that pours down blessings
from your hand

gold coins
one of them is the sun
in the cave of my heart.

South Fallsburg, NY, November 1991

CANDLEMAS (1)

One drop of nectar rolled down
the throat of the giant red amaryllis
and waited at the edge, the sun
rose red over snow
and the phoebe sang out sweetly
her return

return of the sun
the arrows and tips of flame
the women in shades of scarlet
and the men, almost skipping in night air
doing a jig to the stars
and Mars, above Aldebaran, crimson

Tell me a story, the old one
about how we used to strip to the waist
to catch the sun, how the crystal daggers
were wanton roses that gouged out
the heart, and caught achingly
in the throat.

Willow, NY, February 3, 1991

35

Epiphany

I sit in the mirror of my life
down corridors
and find myself not guilty
I see cells separating from the main body
cells detaching themselves
as in holding a vase,
the cells in the hand and in the vase
commingle, then disengage

In the basement of my desire I find
myself fearful
I need my brothers near me
my sisters to cover my back
The significance of gestures
derives from old rituals
I gather the universe to my breast
and let it go

In the vestibule of delirium
I celebrate the child
who remains a child until she dies
and the crone
who has known, from cave and cave
since the beginning how things would turn
The altar piece of her desire!
She lets it fall out of her hand
and roll down the hill

I celebrate the wife,
the happy mate, the closed marriage

of my body to myself or somebody else
I see air being poured into air
from coffer to coffer, the cells
disengage from contiguous surfaces,
the wife comes along and wipes them clean

Married to herself, the wife invents
partners, kinsmen
kinswomen in the common tribe
the helpmeet orders her disarrayed
universe, pouring air into air
and water into water

Woman of the woods walks out
she marches
keeping her eye on the forests
across the way, the tilt of snow
and leavening of sunlight, tiniest maple
flowers begin their dance
spring in the known world, and now
who are you? Where have you been?

The old gestures derive from rituals
we will never forget
we were there and we remember
Walk out into the morning
succeeding brilliantly with small tasks
until the universe— systole, diastole—
breathes in once more, and you are
swallowed. Gather the universe up
and in a gesture of grandest largesse, let it go

Heads and shoulders roll across
the landscape, the sun dial impeccably
recording time

in the tribe we hug each other hard
and pledge to help
the crook of the arm melts into horizons
we promise to help, we stood in close
proximity to each other, sucking up warmth
and food, we promised

Inexorably the seasons marched over the land
the husbandwoman, tender of vines
watched over her crop
she had something to learn
she crawled along the underbelly of desire
dipping her hands in and out
of the known world, reaching
into the flesh and gathering up whole
handfuls of it, like shoe polish

She visualized herself
free of tendrils roots and stem
blushing in the March sun, naked
and surprised
the handmaiden of pleasure
servant of desire
gathered the universe to her breast
and let it go.

Willow, NY, April 1988

POLISH CANTINA

If you don't know what
your name is, how
can I introduce myself?
A boat steams up the shallow river
as though some great port
were in sight, while we stand
in the rushes wringing our hands

Laminated green, the spears
of flowers and leaves separate into
red blue purple yellow
breathing like the accordion
at a Polish wedding
banging our spoons on the glasses
we ask for a kiss
a sign of endearment
the accordion plays into the night

A wet florid quilt of grasses,
tendrils in long-stemmed glasses,
claws on the windshield wipers,
the push and pull of pillars
changing places
right is blue, left is red
The Polish accordion has gotten
everyone off their chairs, onto the dance floor
into each other's arms.

Woodstock, NY, November 1988

39

EROTICA

I

Clouds pass over, animate, inanimate
wind calls
where is the erotica in this?

mother of animals
understanding all languages
speaks in the low voice of knowledge
like Melampus
who hears the termites in oak pillar
"Get out of the house, Melampus,"
they sang,
"we are taking it down."

open the forest in the brain
and the bears come in
listen to the voice of laurel
a green dark sea
and birds fly in, they enter your eye
erotica comes with the draped hill
running through a pine forest
the snap snap snap of twigs as you go
the buttocks of Artemis dappled
in the forest sun

they were in a cave or temple
there were no writings on the wall
they were on a low divan

40

wide enough for the two of them
the oak trees rustled
lips opened to the tongue darting
in and out

write erotica
dancers rolling in pleasure
all the way down the hill
water air and waves of green
song in the high oaks
in the mirror is not existence
no corroboration of spirit

in the dance it is
the dog rolling in the grass
a distance of elements as they coalesce
separate, roll down the hill
a chorus of voices
not yesterday and not tomorrow
having come this far and laughed
this long, says the mother of animals
I absolve you of all impediment
to joy

where is the erotica in this?
in the scratch of straw the calm of leaves
cells drenched with themselves
in the stretch of instep
the wild abandon of the woods
they came upon a grove, a hidden thing
the silky grass they lay on
licking and sucking and sweating
in the shaft of sun

in the vine trembling

and the breath taken by your lover
walls collapse
the mud turtle's mating song
a grunt as he lunges forward
the tap tap tap of their shells
and the frogs
long skeins of eggs in the shallow pool
green over red he clings to her
in the river current

II

In Eros, not everyone answers
it's my life, she says
pointing to herself

a giant night moth
flapping in the puddle of downtown Bogotá
would surely die
they stood transfixed in the glow he gave off
black and gold
powerless to help him

Come to my aid, Eros!
wind means more to the sweating back
help me leap the hurdle
of intuition!

chart a course for me through the wilderness
of crows
loud crows in the afternoon
and no signposts, no fences, no boundaries

No adjunct of anyone else
I am the culprit, the hangman
with covered face, the unexplained presence
at the guillotine of a shaft of light

To drown in the other and not
come up again
O baskets! O mixing jars!
I am the essence in burial urns

The scented wax
and trail of Eros
climbs through the woods and pastures
a faint phosphorescence

I could weep blood, but the drops keep
dancing round the fire
transfigured, dancing, dancing

III

Into the window of the world
enter leaf layers, erotica of green
the busy air, a hummingbird
at the white flowers on the fence
birdcalls through the cathedral
grapevines covering everything
all histories are false stories
a holding to personality
or any particular place on the planet
transient

erotica is desire
the color and fusion and profusion
of desire
profusion of leaves
still in a still place
in hallways of darkened sight
the eyes, accustomed to near places
are taken by the immensity
the body arching up
in fluid access

the fish shaped cloud
over the hillside
a table of ancient objects
we can hardly define
anthem like the tail of a wave
runs through us all
hardly had we begun to arrive
when we were going
whirling into simultaneity
synchronous with the stars
erotica in the wide open eyes.

Willow, NY, July 1988

44

SICK ROOM

Without leaving this bed I am traveling
from Indian summer to the fall
suddenly it's a brisk morning in
November, Paris, high white clouds
over the Seine
yesterday, in this convalescent room
off the porch, where the books
and magazines pile up,
I was in Colombia
just the end of summer, the foliage
glowing richly, reddish green

The happy dog on our hill, killed
yesterday by a car, is replaced by
spiders at her food dish in the garden
the ducks I hear replace the hummingbird
delicate bean plants vie for space with
the sturdy cabbage. I'm flying
with my left fist stretched before me
Wonder Woman penetrates the skies,
my hair streaming behind me as I enter
fall, land softly on the porch, survey
the body with her bruised wound on the bed

Begonias drop red flowers
one by one
I pick them up and place them
on the altar; in a crystal this room
would be red, black, gold
and white

through the left-hand corner of the window
is an empty quadrant, a space of sky
with clouds like sheep
that's enough, that raise of the hem
to keep me busy

The placement of my body for least
distress is a major strategy
pain, the archenemy, yields after time
to boredom; in the unused limbs
are seeds of disaffection
we survey the troops for signs of treason,
of leaving us as they travel on their own
sniffing the air for adventure
I grab the helm off the Irish coast
a crone with bare knuckles, I light the fire
and sail into the dark.

Willow, NY, September 19, 1992

POSTCARD FROM SLOVAKIA

We are in the Esperanto Club,
a nineteenth century solid stone building
at the top of the hill, by the church
in Sobodsky Namesti.
All the uncles I never knew, recipients
of Basia's packages to Poland,
long lean men with superior attitudes,
their hands and clothes full of smoke,
pass by on the street

Their manner on greeting a stranger
is formal and three times respectful,
looking at the ground, the knees, the throat
and then the eyes
Perhaps they'd prefer not to greet me
at all, but go about the cold
hard business of surviving in a world
without lettuce, spinach, or watercress
and no desire for greens

They prefer, it seems, the solidity of pork
With fatty white spots beneath their eyes
they push through the cold persistent rain
like cattle to the warm mammalian barn
at evening, homing in on the meat and beer
and cigarette smoke in pubs
at the end of the tram lines

I wish I could push through the language
and break down the walls

I wish the attraction I felt could be voiced
in other than body language
so the incoherent man who chased me
down the street from the pub, because I guess
he had something to say, and stood
gesticulating wildly, could have a reply

I would point out how much he looked
like Uncle Jack
and tell him the stories I've been told
of the early days in Bayonne, New Jersey,
the moving business with horse and wagon
1920, the dusty streets
the hardworking arms of the men and women,
I would grab him by the arm and call him
brother, cousin, friend.

Sobodsky Namesti, Poprad, Slovakia, April 1990

Basia: Grandmother in Polish

OUT OF THE REACH OF CHILDREN

I've seen them from train windows
        buses, planes
It's hard to miss a nuclear plant
        the eye drawn to the alien shape
of nuclear chimneys squatting on the landscape

I tell kids, Listen,
        you're inheriting a rotten pie.
These nuclear plants are making a poison
        that stays alive for thirty thousand years.
A room full of shocked eight year old faces.

One girl says, Who is doing this?
        It's dangerous. Let's tell them to stop.
A bunch of old men decide, I say.
        They think it's okay.
A boy stands up. He can't believe it.
        Don't they care about us?
        What about *their* children?
        Don't they have children?

Dear Nuclear Commission: Don't you have children?
        Or grandchildren? What about them?
Dear power brokers: Why do you want to sell
        your kids into slavery, cleaning up
        this mess?
A megaton medicine bottle squats
        on the bathroom shelf, with skull
        and crossbones:
KEEP OUT OF THE REACH OF CHILDREN!

Dear energy brokers and racketeers:
        You're running out of virgin forests
        and hidden fields to squat with your plants
You're running out of Third World countries
        to strong-arm into taking your waste
There's nowhere left to turn
        and no one left but us
And we are the children your mother
        warned you about
The ones who would say no
        and we say it: N O   M O R E   N U K E S
And we mean it.
                    N O   M O R E   N U K E S
And we mean it.

We are the children taking back
our mother from your hands.

Prague, Czechoslovakia, April 1990

50

CHILD

Yesterday there was a baby born
in the empty helmet of flowers
and trees
chalky dangerous shadows slid
through the streets
tall ships and warehouses
loomed on the corners

she was born and placed on my shoulder
before she began to feed
she was a cat
three days later she was a little girl
speaking Spanish, asking for her mother
her wild unnatural innocence
the pocket of our home

crime stopped
burly delinquents and their shadows
homed in on the manger, a small
apartment on a broken street
Patres familias, the men were protective
we wore no clothes, tracing our genealogy
in the roots of our hair

her grandmother was the most insistent
we took many buses to get to her
they were having a special deal
and drove to her door
she recounted the first days the child
already knew her own name

the girl jumped up on my shoulder then
wearing somebody else's clothes
I walked down the stairs.

Willow, NY, July 1990

Travel Song

for Alex

I am singing to you, my friend
intent is everything
I've lit a candle, burnt cedar
sage and sweet grass
and even without water I've come
traveling
you are on your feet

singing, I encounter you in a garden
at night, clipped hedges
a solemn moist cool night
I lose my thread and return
again and again
you are dressed in white and walking
calmly, your spirit is not disturbed

I've come to paste healing on your forehead
a poultice of love like an oval heart
I should mention the color blue
a transference of light
not me and you exactly
but mes and yous we have been once
among others

my song sounds like a wailing woman's
in the market place
or a monastery, at a wall, some
former time, the singing is my intent

53

to be with you
here in the garden where we see each other
and walk without a word.

Willow, NY, March 8, 1991

NEWS OF A RIVER
SOMEWHERE ELSE
1989–1993

THE TRIBES

In the ancient plaza we stand
in the dust
in Kathmandu, the old city
and Lima, the city translated
over oceans
to impose a new cruelty
Why are the soldiers gathered here?
Crosses and swords on our continent,
why are they gathered?

We sing in the plaza
despite the pressure of the great ones,
the owners of apparent universes,
we sing and salute ourselves
in our own small perimeters and gardens
Our two-steps, four-steps,
why do you think we dance like this?
In the knowledge that it is
not as you say,
O terrible owners!

The second floors of our houses
are steamy with accumulated
heat
we make love on the straw
on the floor boards
if there are beds, on the beds
we make love despite
your shouts of war, your garbled hymns
of dominion

We call out the names
of the things we love: the sun
coming up around us, moonrise
over the stones, the vegetables
on market day, our children laughing
in the little square
where the troops are gathered now
with swords
where the troops are gathered

And we stand at dawn
our hearts beating against the still air
uncertain if we will live
till nightfall, mother,
if we will live.

Lima, Perú, August 1989

HEARTLAND

for Raúl, Giannina, and the black stones of Huacho

We can track down the old patterns
through customary alleyways,
the way we take our beer in the cafe
for instance, always at room temperature
the way we lie on the left side
gathering in our infancy

This is my home. Isn't it likely
I would be happy here?
I work, I laugh, I love
I meet friends, we work together
I walk the immense earth under this sky
I am not satisfied

I forgot the carriage jostling
along the cobblestone bridge, its interior
full of wheels, the clanking irons
mechanically splendid
lie like snakes
engorged and stretched out on the sand

Where will we sleep?
Did you make a bed for me?
Did you think of me when you fondled
your jeweled casket?
A bundle of wheels lurches into the market
and none of us discerns its purpose
or direction

59

I prefer the threadbare rugs
and stained tablecloths of old tearooms
I prefer the communal disgrace
of garbage heaps
and maggots the size of your thumb
the land black for miles with vultures

I prefer it to the geometry
of prayer
the nodding and naming without belief
the failure of Eros to compel us
the clanking wheels of obsolescence

I prefer the primitive belief in breakfast
the sound of cattle
shuffling feet in the dirt
and the ladder to our sleeping room
where a crescent moon moves across
the window

We dream of snakes coiled and stretched out
on the beach, we lay our towel down
to sleep among them
the sound of clanking wheels is drowned
in the tide receding and the growling stones.

Miraflores, Lima, Perú, September 1989

Musician

Now that you have walked down
        the stairwell, trailing your shadow
and the music you left alive in the air
        is silent, I shut off
the lights, like the careful mother
        of the child inside herself
Our little banquet is broken down
        and eaten
and the cupboards again hold their
        cheese and olives,
The lights are warm in the sheltered
        room, and you walk
on a damp street, fog on the streetlights,
        your shoes creaking in the quiet.

I think of the joy you bring,
        your life lit up with the constancy
of rhythm, I think of your profile
        laughing with the men in the band,
and in that moment, it is as you say,
        no time exists but the present
no other love but the music
        no impulse but your hands
inside her
        echoing down a spiral stairway
where no shadow touches your face
        no shadow touches your face.

Angel is a body of light.
		Your face lit up, your missing
finger, your laughter, your Afro haircut,
		The fingerprints of your persona
are lines in a piece of music
		stretching out to the horizon,
staccato, coming back in
		And you are the dancer
across the page, alive in the air
		where no shadow touches your face
hermano,
		no shadow touches your face.

Miraflores, Lima, Perú, September 1989

TAULLIRAJU

I throw myself on the ground
at fifteen thousand feet, facing
the glacier
and tell myself
people pay thousands of dollars
to trainers to feel this way

I walk so slowly, grandmother
burro, I make myself tired
What's the hurry?
The shine of Taulliraju
is brighter than the bleached skulls
fallen below

I have my story
of the flea who came fishing
last night, and caught me
in my sleeping bag
Stepping over immensities
what a feast he had of legs, stomach
and thighs!

Step by step make of your life
an act of love
said my friend, the poet
and first I am the mother
who loves herself
then I am the mother who loves
everyone else

and I am the flea
permitted to feast
on immensity after immensity
permitted to cross the pass
I hope
and feast on the other side.

Glacier Taulliraju, Callejón de Huaylas, Perú,
August 1989

BATHTUB

Leaning over the flat rocks
in the river
fifteen minutes more of sun

one little bird
sets up a cry
from the slopes of the glacier

avalanche on the left
and right, hot sun
a perfect bathtub

the woman naked
under the sky contemplates
the water, sexual from the inside out

like herself
the woman inside the woman
loves herself, smiles over the river

bent waist down
in the secret spilling
over the containments of herself

what a song we sing
of love and onions
birds chirping

on the skirts of the cerro
wind
deep voice of the avalanche

wild acceptance
love what a song
we sing.

Morococha, Callejón de Huaylas, Perú,
September 1989

HUALCAPAMPA

The ácaca bird who flies in the puna
has the ivory beak of a woodpecker
but she hammers her holes in rocks
to make her nest
they say she knows the herb up here
that melts the stones

they say she showed it
to the Inca
who moved his mountains
and worked them to fit so easily
together

The fox has a power
to take away human speech
from the moment he spots you
and you spot him, until he leaves
you can't speak
he makes you stupid
he has the power in his tail

Let's smoke a cigarette
at the doorway to this valley,
advise the spirits that we are here
let's ask permission
to enter the place, ask for their help
in reaching the pass two
days away.

Hualcapampa, Marcará, Perú, September 1990

Ulta

Climbing the switchback at 15,000 feet
strolling in the altitude
flow, don't push
say the waterfalls
and rivulets
I realize I love to walk among these peaks
not on them, not over them
among them
as though I had been walking
in this cape against the weather
just like this for thousands of years

I sit on the edge and watch the play
of clouds among the peaks, the armies
of rain, the sun burning through
illuminating slopes
and fissures that look like sticks in the snow
the roar of water and avalanches
breaks the silence

I realize the fox is my friend and ally
I ask his aid
I jump down a tiny hole and start dancing
down the tunnel, side to side
he runs with me, he covers my belly
with pelts, he lets me mount on his shoulders
we fly over moony landscapes
and I make it to the next switchback
the next waterfall
the next tumult of rain

my heart opens like a plum
and light pours out
I'm connected to the prints I leave
and the fresh ones of the fox on the road
and the holes in the ground
and the other fox at my side, behind me.

Ulta mountain, Callejón de Huaylas, Perú,
September 1990

The Pass

Up the last slope before Ulta Pass
at 16,000 feet, our stopping place
a grotto of falling icicles
the landscape is a lithograph

of black, brown, gray, and white
Coming to the pass, there's no way over
a recent landslide
the rocks still poised to roll

No tunnel no road no donkey trail
just a smell of sulphur
blood on the snow
a menacing pile of boulders moving

People up above are pointing
Easy that way, they say,
Easy this,
Easy for them to say, they're not down here.

Ulta Pass, Callejón de Huaylas, Perú,
September 1990

AUQUISMAYO

The startling good news of this waterfall
is the fly walking over the rock
in the sunlit spray
and the grass who has lost her vicious
claws to the rain, and is tender
reflecting green

I have an alliance with these people
of the Andes
much like Synge on the Aran Islands
I love them, I respect them
I will never be them
nor they me

Our regard for Pachamama
is the same
I sing to her, they work with her
we are open we observe we love her
yes I can say that
we love her

The compelling good news of this waterfall
is how vitally alive we run
splashing jumping leaping
rock to rock
no need of watchers
the sun and shadow are equal to us

the leaves the trees the lands we pass
violence tenderness
equal to us.

Auquismayo, Callejón de Huaylas, Perú, September 1990

Fox Song

Well, little fox
your charms are paid for

Wind at the top of the seventh cerro
a sear wind
of hawk and ácaca bird

The desert opens my solar plexus
to vegetal calm
the death component
in thorn bushes and stony ground

Didn't I find your bones on the trail?
Didn't I pick them up for a rattle
with the dry seeds of *salta perico*?

We haven't come so far from the ruins
on the ridge
to this abandoned corner

A turtle's voice wakes up
in the dead leaves, the wind bringing news
of a river somewhere else

Deer startled in his haven, ácaca
preening on her rock, one drop of water
so precious to the throat

Like the laughter of someone running away
little fox
with the voices he stole.

Condormarca, Callejón de Huaylas, Perú, September 1990

72

A Gift of Flowers

for Glicerio

You ask if I remember the flower
you gave me last year
on the puna, called *Rima Rima*

more than the flowers
I remember myself
on this or that mountain

but the flower you put in my hat just now
from the cactus *Huácuru Huayla*
with a stick through the center
to keep it open

drones like a bumblebee
in the wind
as I run down the hill.

Vicospampa, Marcará, Perú, September 1990

73

DOORWAY

I can understand the houses
built with no windows
and only one door

and the door
facing into a closed courtyard
of flowers, water jugs, and drying meat

After all day walking in the vastness
clothed in space, with the wind
to talk to

you want to come in
where it's dark and warm
and everyone knows your name.

Yumani, Island of the Sun, Lake Titicaca, Bolivia,
August 1993

ISLAND OF THE SUN

When horizons are blurred
and you cannot see where
shore and sky meet

you could be on any island
off the Irish coast,
in the Aegean Sea

a line of sailboats
leaves the port
in a stiff wind from the north

and all enclosures
seem like a waste
of time

they round the lighthouse
at the tip of the lizard's tail
and fan out

there will be fish
in all the kitchens
tomorrow.

Island of the Sun, Lake Titicaca, Bolivia,
August 1993

Kitchen Dream

In my room over the kitchen
in Barranco, the shadow of incense
curls across the wooden floor
I lean over the kingdom
of my possessions, and just like that
one day
the smoke will stop

A pigeon lands outside my door
and coos, coming in and
out of silence
like a life
lit up for a moment
like someone at the mouth of a river
rushing out to sea.

Barranco, Lima, Perú, September 1993

76

Plaza de Armas

I make my way
a rocking boat down the pavement
penicillin poisoned
swollen joints
my neck stiff with anchors

I am slowly circling, waiting
for the moon
waiting for the face of Huascarán
waiting for an homage of flowers
to sit in, and watch
the sunset

Huascarán wears
pink
on the last skirt of glacier
There are two ways to do it:
one is to sit and love and watch,
the other is to climb.

Huaraz, Perú, September 1993

77

Thermal Baths of Chancos #5

I came to see you
in your brilliant heat
and I got angry

at your unkempt altar,
I waded through dead eucalyptus leaves
acacia branches, stepped over
shampoo packets

only
looking back
I called you, Kali Durga

in the dark cave
Kali Durga, mother
my mother, your limestone knees

and iron ore, washed
in the heat of volcanic waters
Kali Durga I sang to the dark.

Chancos, Quebrada Honda, Ancash, Perú,
September 1993

POWERS OF THE PLACE

It's no accident
ácaca, that you come
to where I am in your province
squatting behind the *taulli* bush,
to say good-bye

It's no accident
that the waterfall
above us, over the rim of the bowl
is drawn by the wind
like a veil across the morning

and the sun rises wide and
grand over the glacier
Yaku Huarmi, Woman of Water,
and the lightning bugs are loathe
to leave the tent

Ácaca, ácaca,
named for your cackle,
ácaca brrrrrr, like laughter
swooping across the cul-de-sac
as the tents fold up

ácaca
posing on the rock
while five condors
circle
some dead thing

the males have the white neck
and white on their wings
from high above us they circle slowly
six seven eight
a dead cow on the ledges

Outside the portals
beyond the shepherd grazing
her sheep and goats, we head down
the ample valley, the ácaca
calls again

I stop in the middle of the road
to find her, yellow vest
under plain brown wings

she will not go beyond this point
Ácaca, ácaca, a little farther
up the slope already.

Quebrada Honda, Ancash, Perú, September 1993

KEEPSAKE

Arid plain, Andean rock face,
you have been the arena
of my life
lesson by lesson, year after year

What can I give
in the face of such generosity?
Nothing small will do

Can I give my heart to a land mass,
to a river?
Does that make me sentimental?
A skull of stone jutting out of the earth
says it makes me human

The sun has set behind the cliff wall
I pick up the yellow stone
still warm
from the sun on the river bank.

You are giving again.

*La Portada, Quebrada Honda, Ancash, Perú,
September 1993*

THE BARD OWL
1975–1979

ROOTS REVISITED

Long row of cribbed houses
startled in their sleep
by a flight of gulls

Old pastures
seamed and paved over
cliffs abandoned to high-rise
apartments
rain soaked cardboard boxes
slide down the hill.

The eye
takes refuge in a wake of birds
from bickering heritage
a cramped continuum
and spotted leaves

A past left long ago
in a graveyard back alley
flight from roots
revisited.

Rubble graces the remains
of a sultry day
November and no winter
in sight. A train of boxcars
rumbles by in the hazy
sun over Hoboken

Land mass soaked
in its homemade steam
to the latitude of southern cities,
Washington and Baltimore,
a rose blooming in November
and a man in his frantic narrow bed
turns over and over.

Thanksgiving over the marsh land
and debris, the roar of traffic
clanking wheels
a bird on an empty park bench
turns his head.

Weehawken, NJ, Thanksgiving 1975

86

THE TRAVELER

for Susan & Martin Carey

Astride a window ledge in the cave
I am careful to surround myself with
the elements for feedback and support
Sitting by the side of a stove at twilight
a tunnel opens in the roof of my mouth
and tenuous fingers disturb the foliage

Here on a spree, on an outing in the home
of myself, I worry over timetables
remember to bring the cracked opera glasses
pick up after myself at every turn
The sky shoots in with its royal purples
and I'm off again

I've tried to pin this down, to surround it
with a mass of evidence, to get concrete results
and nothing works. A sputtering candle fills me
with the certainty of a click of fate heard
lately in a dream, and sure as my knees at the
sideboard, it's an omen, a reminder

A dim horn in the distance calls me
over fields and rounded hills to a gathering
of plenty. I see there are no notices in the paper,
nor are the walks of normalcy disturbed
No snow crackles under the traveler's feet
out walking without a body, senses peeled
like an apple to the deer nibbling down the sky.

Woodstock NY, January 1976

87

WINTER

It is five in the morning
I drive over icy roads
at a sane and reasonable speed
Hazardous turns and corners
rear up in the headlights
cold hands drum on the bones

I am not fooled
into considering you
as ominous dark tyrant
danger-headed and
full of holes

In the cracks
and corridors of windswept
alleys I am not fooled
Prominent over the old hills
rise the horns of the moon
familiar pastures
sea voyages, the fixed stars

Give me your winter
fixed like a wooden shoe
at the fireplace,
slightly blackened,
I am not fooled

The shoe
after many trials and oilings
fits the awkward musculature,

I stalk the woods in
animal skins, wearing
your night like a glove.

Woodstock NY, January 1976

Song for the Lady

The lake to the east was green
they say a lady came out of the hills
rubbing her eyes
A silver mast in the near waves
powdery branches on the shore
They say a lady came out of the water
rubbing her eyes.

Do not be deceived by her rounded eyelids
heavy with sleep
the clicking of aspen leaves under water
Her salt mill grinds away, amassing treasures
conjuring webs and delicate foliage
patterns of frost on the windows
do not be deceived
The earring in her left ear is the brightest
She is gathering treasure.

Over the hills to the east
comes a pink dawn, shells are strewn
in layers on the shore
She comes out rubbing her eyes
a golden earring pierces the fog bank
pale deer foraging through snow drifts
mauve and green.

She is coming over the snow with her salt mill
over the surface tension of water
a thin bird, mosses delicate and waving

Do not be deceived by her carriage
seven league boots are frail
next to her footsteps.

Woodstock NY, January 1976

HERE AT THE DOOR

for my father, Joseph Pommy

I

Your face turned to the side in the kitchen,
we talked of death
I didn't know it would be
you, your tired gaze over the table

Everywhere I've been asked to choose
and wouldn't
Every frail place with humanity on its knees
that I passed over,
wishing now perhaps that I had stayed
and glanced back in complicity
and didn't

Once with a boy in a dark room
young myself, I felt
it was you there with me making love
and I sent you a letter, a loveletter
raving about a man with red hair
you said when you saw me
you did not understand.

I feel like a river
a wide river in the morning
birds and fish move over and through me
tenacious with life, each own little life,

92

and there is no bridge that spans me
no shore in sight.

I came in that last night to an empty
house, the living room darkened,
I leaned my head against the wall
and thought I felt a soul buried there,
beating to get out, and thought of my mother
through years in that room, the narrow
confines, now in the hospital,

I sat down to write you a letter.
There were things I could not put on paper
You came in then, and we sat at the table.
I can feel death coming, I said,
and thought of my mother.

Death leaves us so disheveled
The private thrashings in a dark room,
the inspection of personal belongings—
Where is a man's life told in his father's
cross and apron?
Where is a man's life told by the blaze
of his hair at a sunny window?
Where is a man's life told by his last
glance over a kitchen basket, saying,

Death, yeah, well ... I'm really tired.

II

Hello.

In my sleep just now
two days after death
Your voice on the phone
before waking

Hello?
As though you expected I'd know
who it was

HELLO.

III

THE LOVE SONG

In my monk's bed I lie down
your room is right next door
your room your bed
the ransacked habiliments of your life
strewn in the corners

I have
left the door open
lit one candle

I suppose in my way I am
sewing a veil a curtain
a doorway

Your way is fixed
as is mine
a path is set
we cannot alter that

A rustling
from in back of the room
the sound of wings
or the hushed cloth of someone in sorrow
reverence or prayer

You out on the wings of the wind
aware of the ceremonious rites

the public
grief turned towards a body
made suddenly our property
We preside like kings at a table

Your vessel the body
offered up
in a barbaric feast of eyes
the clay the cold
and weathered flesh
the veined familiar hands

Love, you strange one,
there is no doubt
the mind may question
the soul in its caparison gaze out

but

love from the solar plexus
urged out like thin
wires on the air
there is no question.

IV

RITES OF THE EASTERN STAR

Ladies reading
from little books
What are they saying?

We sit
in the first row holding hands
the family of this man
in the coffin
the privileged watchers
in velvet chairs, the scrutinized,
the bored and visiting royalty

I warn you we must have
passion! Open the flood gates!
The merciless seas!

The rigid semicircle
of women in white uniforms
fans out in front of the coffin
clutching flowers, dogmatic verse
they give us a tepid theater piece,
vague sermons hang in the seams
of their garments. Give us
violent theater, I tell you!
Draw back the curtains!
Release the hounds!

The great tragedians
knew how to wring the necks of swans
you could hear the cracking of bones
from the seventh row—
stories of man on his bleeding knees
before irrevocable fate,
his fight with the sea
Give us strict and passionate
tragedy! The mighty chorus!
The inconsolable line!

Tepid verse read from dog-eared
manuals in wooden voices
will not serve.
If we wanted scraping chairs
and muffled coughs
we could have gone to the movies,
sat with old Chinese insomniacs
in ancient North Beach theater, watching
Tom Mix moving somnolent
through a restless fog.

Give us passionate screams
in your chorus!
Wailing women in a thick night!
Murderous seas!

The greasy fingers
of the king, displeased,
crack another neckbone.

V

MASONIC RITES

The rustling from in back of a room,
a gathering of tribes in lambskin
aprons. Every man's suit is crimped
at the waist, breaking the symmetry
of his armor, making him somehow
vulnerable to the fates
They carry the tools of their trade
a mallet stuck in the waistband,
the square and level about the throat,
two men with staves at the coffin
Like kings around a table
they cover the room.

This is the play inside the play
the ritual we hoped for
A man looks into our eyes and speaks
of mansions, looking through a glass
darkly, but then face to face. If it
were not so I would have told you.
The speech I often heard you recite
yourself in your darkened bedroom.
Everyone here, accustomed to your
part in the play, is listening inside
himself for your voice. I feel you
also behind us, listening.

Each man approaches the coffin
alone, turns to it and
speaks softly. The body there
appears a grim personage
You are behind us
They are saying good-bye.
The young, the vigorous and longhaired,
the old, infirm, hunch-shouldered,
the ones in wheelchairs,
one by one they pass and stand
one by one they salute the death
we carry inside.

I see the towering brotherhood
behind them, stretching back
to corridors, lecterns, circles
temples built in the form of man
and the ones who worked in
stockinged feet, the sons of the Mother.
A muffled tread sounds through the temple
proximity to death lifts up a curtain
we glimpse the workings of the wheel
in seconds, tenths of seconds—
your voice on the phone this morning,
Wheels, I tell you! Radiant wheels!

VI

A candle lit
the crowded furnishings
of an empty cell

Your body
burned in an upright furnace
on a sunny day

The stick
that held up your window
lies on the sill

My mother
frail in her brief clothes
against the night the unknown
warp and woof of death
sits in the kitchen
watching tv for the sound of it
a little comfort

I stay
constraining passions to a mild
hoof beat in the distance
wait
for the terrible horses
to ravage the door

This pageantry of death,
you must be pleased,
you strange one

The lifting of ornate curtains
cosmic gowns, the bare delineament

of pathos in the shoulder muscles
hunched against the night, against
the horrible details of loss

your not being
ever again
where I could see you.

My mother laughs and is comforted
she has
her daughter for the night
anaesthetized beyond hope of doors
opening or closing
in the kitchen she sits and laughs
she has
her daughter for the night.

O radiant tower
valiant lions of change
instill in me your ardor
your inevitability

When the time comes
bring me comfort in the darkened corner
empty of a wall
a pillar
empty
of a place of birth

One candle and a thin bed
sail the night.

Weehawken NJ, April 1976

102

The Voices

Something under the bones is calling
dragging me down to the root of myself
I stop on street corners
taking telephone numbers from men
who could be lovers, it does not change
I seek out every face I've ever loved
as carrion, food for the bones
it only widens the crease to a
scar on the waters
If bones were soft, it would be
in the bones. This is under that,
like a sea on a flooded meadow.

I have grown lean and bend with the wind
like a green stem whose flower is
plucked waves in the grasses
I look covertly for promises from total
strangers in the street, the soft place
under the bones dark and rippling,
Murmuring sounds like the lowing
of cattle far off over the hills
move through my footsteps
As though I could equate the bricks on both
sides of an alley with the sliding through
and still not reach the yard

My body gravitates toward darkened corners,
foxholes where the wounds are licked
and licked again
The worker wanders from her tools and is found
sitting in a chair with limp hands
watching the rain slide down the window
A valley of quiet graves in the moist ground
murmurs under root and footstep,
hovering over the sound is a mother buried
inside me, her bare arms cover the sea.

Weehawken NJ, May 1976

SPRING

Curtained night the muffled
door the wet leaves
hungry
swallowing footprints

fields are camouflaged
enclosure to the eye
two eyes
in two directions

Who would suspect the owl
the mystic owl, of yearnings?
Why don't we
call the soul a dog

for crooning at the hills?
Or a scuttling beetle
dark-faced
in a galaxy of horses.

NYC, May 1976

"galaxy of horses" from J.Gonzalez's poem "Death."

Song for César

César Vallejo, the bridge of your nose,
I lean on a parapet in Lima
and think of your fierce unyielding face
in Paris, the 1930's, your cheekbones
like stone terraces in the little park

It is drizzling. The sound of traffic
dies after midnight
One lamppost lights the pages of
your notebook. You sit hunch-shouldered
collar up against the rain
or against intrusion
settling into the brooding crags
Who can see your hawk eye
penetrate the corners of the night
full of love and murder?

In the gray dawn you are still there
writing, even though it is raining
The furrows between your eyes
frown into the distance
Workmen pass with their lunch pails
and noisy laughter, you do not see them
Your wife watches from a gray window
across the street. *Look at the angel,*
she says, *the madman*
who never comes home to sleep.

You will not yield until the gaze comes
back full circle from its horizon, and
lands like a bird on the wire fence.

Then you close your book and walk
to the steamy cafe.

Lima, Perú, June 1976

PANAMA AIRPORT

Desolation sits in a fluorescent
airport at 3 a.m.
seamy wash buckets crowd the john
an old lady nods at the washbowl

Taciturn answers find meet response
The luggage wheel bangs on
a sordid eternal cast
settles over the baggage

Bones are buried at deserted crossroads
winds howl, dark
halved chickens are offered up
the blood dried on the feathers

The traveler passes through corridors
of duty-free goods, obscene at this
hour, and a waiting room where
a woman sleeps tied to her suitcase.

The only animal fit to survive here
must be man,
his temples built to resemble
himself, the willful
portions of his brain
where he labored blindly

Only the earth could turn out
generous enough
to swallow the whole
and leave the splinters

Only the vast green fields
absorb
and somnolent, forget him.

Panama, July 1976

TRAIN RIDE

for Hugh Delehanty

The afternoon elongates
blistered roots of black oak, manzanita
crack the earth
somnolent hills pass, white and crackling
the desert of our humanity stands
with dry palms at a window

Greens in the passing trees hold
glimpses of a home I've never seen
and look for, feet pushing into the earth
like soft mud, sucked in there
and rooted

Houses with tin roofs built in a day
when beauty was abandoned
pass by, roads I've never walked down
wind away
Where is the path my feet will find
immediately familiar?
Where will my body lean
on a sleepless night, a night of revelry
the stars sticking to my shoulder blades
and like a horse, be led home?

I have passed over continents
attentive to a chord struck
in the body

Language childhoods melt away
and I lean out over the edge of a cliff
a tuning fork in the wind
to wake on another day perhaps
when the tide went out and I sat there
empty, examining my hands

I watch how the pages curl in a book
I've scrutinized for thirty years
often the illustrations are blurred
and I turn to a chapter written
in an unknown tongue, and stand there
rooted, ridiculous and certain.

California, July 1976

The Empress

for R.S.

Today at sundown there was
a moment when Venus
shone out of the west
and the moon rose into a cloud bank
on the eastern mountain
The music they played
at the wedding rang in my ears

You bring with you such tenderness
the minutes alive then
with such valor
sitting in an afternoon
watching the valley spread out below

There is more to this,
a victory I cannot name
assurance of an animal walking
the forest, offering up
all gestures with a staid grace

One can only imagine such selfless
stance before the winds of change,
inhabit the seat we find on the path
as a throne, a providential
dwelling place, the animals

112

grouped together in the barn
the wet fur steaming
witnessing in awe a light
that glows inside the body
like a child.

I feel I walk down
ancient halls, no sound of footsteps
disturbs the passage
diving down to a place
I always remembered.

It is the one within us
we approach as a mask, to wear
her from the inside, to be worthy
of such radiance, surefooted
among the stars, to wear a cape
inherited with the genes

The possibility of everything
touched
to grow into that light
that spreads within itself, has always
lived there as a seed.

Shady, NY, November 7, 1976

The Lover

With you it is so easy
taking off leaf by leaf
watching them fall

I address a constancy in your gaze
a long broad avenue of seeing
though I come with forgetfulness
or averted face

I've been so long attentive
like the madwoman on her couch
who would not give up
In her furnished room for years now
newspapers piled to the ceiling
she would not stir, she would not
open the door, she was waiting

The space I live in curves with me
I have set it like a stage
the stars are witness, just back
from the edge of the cliff
Sometimes I sit and stare
at the walls. The leaves are
green and silver when they fall.

Shady, NY, January 1977

THE REGULAR

for Billy Twigg

Memory of other times
the stop gap
short stop glitter

Glamour till it turned
again to a dry
mouth in the morning

Memory of former times
the dreamer in a candid shot
the frail inventions

Short stop stop gap glitter
as in all that shines
et cetera

No penumbra Jack of Doom
cave down the walls
exacerbation

A wanton floating glance is all
fixed coldly on the gold dust
as it falls.

Truth in the tale
that as one is seen, so is
that one empowered

Pacing a cave bereft
of psychic glamour, glitter
in the bank account closed down

from lack of grace,
the lone nun in her cell
without communion

Bring your bankroll!
Glittering green gold serpent glances
up from under

Steam rising from the dancers
on a cold night
feeds the wanton lover!

Sportsman Tavern, Mt. Tremper NY,
January 1977

The Birds

for Armando

We are vast birds of prey, you and I
the stars shining through your cheekbones
blue of your hair in shadow,
birds of prey that rush out
over the ground with the sound
of wheels, or the twisters in Kansas

And one is known by the tail feathers
glimpsed through a crack in the door
The flicker of a black night
seen in the back of an eye before
it blinked
and looked away

Powers inhabit the space
we move in. Shadows cover the ground
at noon, the moon at night
is more than the moon, mountains
stop in the air and listen

They are gathering momentum
like great wheeling birds
with black feathers
There is no turning against
the wind of their wings

Hand signals leap from the dancers
one to the other
Vast and starry knees
straddle the sky.

Shady, NY, April 1977

118

THE HERMIT

Something reminiscent of a barren plain
is what I dreamt of
no oppressive foliage drowns the chest
no tropical abundance, no thousand
tiny murders
but the quick clean kill of condors
their wind-burned plummet
through the edges of the sky
like cosmic scavengers

What I had in mind was a lake
in the middle of a fierce horizon
beautiful mountains on all sides
a population of owls, and the nightly
slaughter of the landscape by
the wind, sun, thirst, and altitude

What I wanted was a place apart
from the smell of mankind
to one by one raze the personal demons
and earn a pure cry
to inhabit this escape and there
whittle down the stances to a dry bleached
skeletal design
to carve a flute from the pelvic bone
whose only fruit is the song it sings.

Shady, NY, May 1977

119

THE BARD OWL

Almost like tears
in the bottom of your eye
like a shade of tenderness
at the kill

As if the tearing claws spread
blood and spirit
merciless in their service
to the Dog Star

As if the claws held night
by the throat
the wolf on one side of the path
the dog on the other
howling at a green moon
and you stood on a hillock
smiling

Swift portrayal of the kill
in the hush of wings
in the great round eyed surveillance
every bush and tree indelibly
combed over

And she came as a woman,
you remember?
Once as a mother, plucking out
the heart strings, tender
merciless she came
wearing jewels

the Dog Star and the Hunter
for a belt
Large eyed and generous
she swooped with beak and talon
mercy dripping from the branches,
you remember?

Silent as the wind
in your eye you service
the lonely chirps in the night
croon to the knees of death
In your great jeweled throat
you carry the night as hostage

Temples have been built and furnished
renovated pyramids and still
you stand on your hillock
with the pang of absence in your jaws
with the roar of cataracts
with the tenderness of tooth and claw.

Willow, NY, May 1, 1977

121

Promise of a Day

Getting off the bus for the thousandth
time in Jersey
footsteps take on the dimensions
of sails over far-off landscapes
vast expanses under my feet move
silently as oarsmen

Venus gone from us, there is in
returning a tattoo of commitment
to the old veins
Red horizons gathered under smoke
the smell of a walker familiar
with the alleys of spring

And somewhere from the past is coming
a day that will not be put aside
that will catch up and pass me
the oars slipping into their locks
with certitude

Somewhere in the past that will not
recede, the embodiment of desire
strikes out on a course
and I stand irretrievably lost
to details and surroundings,
soar with the wings of one
swallowed

122

Eye stare out
from the neck feathers, blind to
restrictions, and bury the night.

Weehawken, NJ, March 30, 1977

THE RITUAL

for my mother, Irene Pommy

I

Your red dress in the coffin
your dead lips sewn together
I'm wailing out in the parking lot,
you would not approve

I look at our friendship
how you served me as loyal back-up
to my vagaries— the confidante,
the faceless friend across the table

how I served you as visiting sister
bringing you eager news from
the outside, bringing you
someone to talk to

We have known each other before.
Only in the working out of fixed
roles, mother and daughter,
did we fail
I serve the life you would not
in yourself.

124

II

Another door is closed
on the past
the tactile childhood comfort
shed like a lizard, the skin
still wet and glistening

Disintegration in a small room
the interlapping voices, grief
debris

I look for a quiet place
to talk
but you are sleeping

I am stark, withdrawn
my mind and body at ebb tide
squat on the sand

What generations of women
am I heir to?
What distillation of knowledge
has come hurtling down
to serve
this soul's design?

Those vestiges
of your personality
hooting around and
looking for a place to roost,
I won't take them home.

III

At the first shock of Daddy's dying
we pulled together for the first time
since childhood,
discovered ourselves
as a family, close-knit, layered
with feelings
but you were there then,
you were always there.

Now we've had practice.
"Second act at nine o'clock,"
my brother calls out.
"Give me fifteen minutes
before show time."
We've had practice.
Like the horse, accustomed
to the lay of the land, and the driver
useless, drunk at the reins,
we can turn the bend impeccably.

IV

Another service
of the Eastern Star,
a dissertation on flowers
"She loved flowers,"
Aunt Helen said,
"looked like a jonquil."

Myself I prefer the masculine
smell of pine needles, moss
over stone and a raging river,
mountains and vertiginous falls

I will not be buried in quiet books
with moth-wing grandmother flowers
will not be pressed into service
as the passive wife
will not sit counting memories
in a darkened corner
resurrect myself with dreams
and stillborn lives

They are saying the prayer
the one about mansions

My crying serves to dispel the loss
of your eyes
your eyebrows
magnified behind glasses
your terrible last year on the planet
the grappling with myself
in you, you in myself
You would not approve.

Weehawken, NJ, July 1977

V

Aer Lingus

Goodbye.
I won't come back waving
at your window, or visit your house
the rooms, end to end, empty
the door ajar

I know as well as you
what I go to find
I carry inside
I am not blind to the uselessness
of travel

A dead board sits
where my heart should be
if you knock on it now
it echoes
I am going away

You're right
I should have been an actress
chosen a role with all the passionate
intensity that returns the day, obliterates
the past, brings the house down

Snip snip snip the scrape of
garden shears out the window
cutting the sky in half

and we can never go back
to where we were

I am leaving in a black night
rigid heart and smog
covering my exit
you will not be at the table
when I return.

Ireland, August 1977

PREVIEW

for Irene Setaro & Bill Pommy

I am entering another time
like the gray film in an old print
moving slowly to the left and gone
I am shouldering a clarity
a stripping away of details
to a bare renewal

I don't know what I will learn by walking
The shock at seeing my body
from an unaccustomed angle in the glass
previews a shuddering into place
of a stance, a knowledge
of my place at a meal

The clarity will not recede
though I bury myself in a charwoman's life
the clean-up crew and cosmic scavenger;
Cups and saucers, furniture
and boxes
do not lessen the intensity of absence

I guess we cry at change
at the child who always had arms
in the wings of the stage, protective
Now the audience is seated, we are broken
in the vessel of what went before
and must come ahead in fact acting
as if we knew

130

I guess we cry at change.
The face of my mother crosses a threshold
intent on what she holds in her hands,
she sits at the table— open
friend of the pure heart!

The luxury of dreaming gone
we improvise in terrible freedom
the role of the ancestors we've become,
the ones onstage with a splendid
curtain rising, leaving an awful light
required to invent the play
make up the parts, live out the end.

Rosses Point, Ireland, August 1977

Your Song

I have not yet sung your song
the one that stands
hard boned, victorious

Passing over the landscape you
stood watching for forty years
your whole adult life,
difficult to see as you did
without dripping into sentiment
to catch the song left
singing in the marshes westward
or in the willow tree outside,

repository of hope, your life
the smell of your bread the last ten years
repository of illness at the end
the firm boned will grown fragile
at the window, the idea you had
that "help would come,"
when it comes from ourselves and you
who taught us that forgot.

Looking at the dynasty of your self
the heirlooms we are left with
intimate touches of that childhood
creasing the center of the brain
creating seeds for the beings
we would become

We were tended by a selfless gardener
the best of herself left growing
around her feet, left
after the hurdles of winter
singing in the wind through the marshes
over the cliffs and down
to the river

your song
strong boned, victorious.

New Jersey, December 22, 1977

133

WALKER

We are most at home on the earth extending
the body beyond itself
The first fear creeping in of turf, root,
body, self, and we stumble
awkward, tenderfooted

Tonight we walk protected by Queen Maeve's
mountain to the west
the bridge at sundown, stone wharves
and walls lean intimate
over the water

Powers are mounted up against denial
The soft sure spin of an easy walker
reeling out her days, a pride
in the pack she will carry away
at nightfall

Like the tramps and tinkers patient
in a ditch at twilight
banking little fires against the night,
we start the stony climb for the windswept
brow of the hill.

Sligo, Ireland, September 1977

JAMESON'S WHISKEY

for Mick Lally

Rack, ruin and a wrinkled brow
immense star patterns
and scuffed boots carry me on

Is it raining? Will the body weave its way
over pavements, tar spots shiny
with the blood of dawn?

You know, you who turn
the handle of a door,
I am fiercely happy in this solitude

Every move ignited by an absolute
self-absorption, a disparate
freewheeling kinship

Broken the lines behind us
of what was known, the windpipes
wired poles, address the dark

I will not come in from the wild night
to familiar grounds
the haunted self-reflection

All grand gestures reduced to a meager
fidgeting and figuring out
tomorrow's meal

I will go on weaving songs
in the dead of night, anonymous
and entirely empty.

Rosses Point, Ireland, September 1977

136

November Landscape

for Maureen Owen

Mauve hills, slate colored sky
offset by the expensive gifts
of virgins—feathered
brooches, jewel encrusted birds
late blooming sumac

Unrelieved gray marble
in the Sultan's vestibule lit up
by a few extravagant fans.

Shady, NY, November 1977

The Geminids

I can see it in the set of furniture
the curve of ornaments against the wall
a stepping off place, from what is
known to what is not
and the body there in its water
swimming
picks up the threads
ferries the mind home listening
for meteors
as though a chord were struck
and one saw it, green
some vast piano.

Shady, NY, December 1977

138

HIMALAYAN AIR IN THE CITY

for Ira Cohen

Odd this night to have risen
to have lost a glove, to have
sunk into mountains, into forests
and the forest's edge

People luminous over thin streets,
quaking bodies, ecstatic hands
two visions of the Tree of Life
from the bat tribe

Show me the bat who is crucified
to his wings
and I recognize
acorn, serpent, seed in the furrow.

In back alleys of the mountain town
we sat crosslegged, calling
the stars by name, the radiant
entities conjoined in a figure eight

and not an eight,
and not conjoined. A cup
with a golden rim.
See? You forgot.

Let me along with ten thousand
deities bless the depths of the forest
lose my glove in a thicket
peer into the well

see no reflection.

NYC, February 1978

140

John Garfield's Favorite Song

for Emmett Grogan

Nail another coffin shut, a face
turned to the wall, another
cigarette consumed
Who do we cry for?

Histories remembered leave us
lonely for our past selves
Watch that gesture leaning into
a curve, flamboyant
stuck in the mind like a thumbprint

Billy Batman, Paula McCoy, now Emmett
in an emptiness
I'd kick in the face if I could, flat handed
waste that leaves the land behind me
rubble, a bleak prospect ahead

Improbable freckles, your ready wit
Oh Lord, won't you buy me a Mercedes Benz
Our snowball fight in the dead of winter,
you nodding almost to your knees
shooting from the second floor window

I celebrate your life
the chances lifted from the fog
the brilliant takes still standing upright
hate to death your love of your own
dark profile on the wall.

NYC, April 6, 1978

141

YOURSELF

I've become a cream puff, a pushover
a patsy. In my dream
we understand each other perfectly
I rake the fields and bring up
hen's eggs, orchids, hearts of gold
Your step becomes buoyant
you stalk the heron, the icy stream
and bring back feathers

I watch you when your gaze goes out,
the wanderer tracking icy steppes
snow mountains, the animal soul
exultant in his skin
A hesitant opening out of gates
on iron hinges
in the garden is a lake, the moon
inside it deep as it is high.

Willow, NY, December 1978

NOCTURNE

for Marilyn

Romance is like a canyon,
echoing off ledge and precipice
are brutal stories, intimations of
rock slides over the field of vision

The wind goes through the walls, it roars
in the left ear— call of a locomotive
to the farm windows late at night, songs
of plunder and anguish

Make love to the unconscious, you could say,
make love to the savage king. We are born
of a race that rides in the night, our breath
is sweet, our reins and grimace a wild
and abandoned dance.

You could plow the fields for jewels
and you would find them. I can hear the cackling
widow with her crown. Her neck
is thin, her laugh is hollow.

Fingers dance in a tiny circle, playing a game
of stones arranged by instinct. Fragments
of a song return, the story of a body of people,
rituals enacted and the heart immersed

You could stand at the window,
watch that one with the feathered coat
rework him into a thousand faces,
but the song you remember

is an anthem of voices
like northern lights that abandon themselves
in synchronicity.

Willow, NY, March 1979

Blue Hills at Dusk

for Huncke

The dreamer, her hand on the plow
her eyes on the furrow ahead
looks off
something is suddenly wrong
with her life, she looks over
silent fields, blue hills at dusk
almost as if the landscape would
provide an answer

The woman at her altar
a cubic stone with
candles
is bent double, her dreamer stopped
weighted down by sky, stone, air
inertia
her tears water paths she will walk down
drop by drop, deserting her past

And the walker, in love with her vision,
the crickets singing her round
the bend, where the best of prospects
awaits her
her dream is off tracking a song she
almost remembers but
cannot hear
and will break every rule to follow

Look at the star lost lover
relegating every comfort to the one
she faces
having put her basket on that rock
she waits in alternate postures:
hope, grief, certainty, despair
and the one who will carry her basket
does not arrive

Think of the voice triangular among us,
the star in the horn of the bull,
speaking calmly to the one beyond
the one you know
consider the roots growing
upside down
in a milky stream, a sea
a hayloft

and tell me,
where is it where is it
where is the one this one
can talk to?

Willow, NY, May 1979

146

HOME

for Charley & Pam Plymell

Cool breeze through the window
the stream runs under pine trees
raccoons plot in the underbrush,
the visitors to this house are old friends
standing under the stars
of enclosed horizon, bounded by trees
and the little forms that govern our daily life
bound by a self with easy access
to its history

There's a song of wolves, where they simply call
and if only we could do that, stand upright on a clear night
calling the stars to witness
the urging of moon rain flesh and again delight
at no fixed place, the hunched over tending
of flickering fire at the onset of a long night.
Laughing with a friend we surrender to that
little place, our hearts
in the dark, our frailty in the thick of it

There are songs belonging to certain trees,
colors unaware of themselves stand in a grove
reticent glowing seashell colors
We sit down to a meal of those same colors
the amber light of a shared eye over the place mat

the night makes convoluted flights
over fixed places, selves in time, and we go back
in our absentmindedness to the home we took
with us and forgot to let go.

Willow, NY, July 1979

RE-ENTRY

for Angus MacLise

You walk out into the night
rail at the stars, you shout through
a year of nights, in the morning
you still wake up, you are
still there

What will you do with your hair
your nails and eyebrows
what will you do with your hair?

Confusion stems from being
too long away
the confluence of stars unrecognized
you look at photos, memories of the mind
and can't return to the places
you might have been

Like sewing the bones up
in their casing, harbored there
affected by tides, floods, tonal changes
the self in absence
the self entrenched in absence

One night the body went out to find
its darkness, it went through swamps
meridians, echoes at the poles
it went knowing nothing but four limbs

loping toward the horizon, finding another place
and walking, calm in the evening
calling the stars by name

A meal of darkness, stripped of its renewal
walked the beach, contemplating skulls cracked
in the fire, the body broken
there was no light but what you thought was light
no clearcut passage, you went blind
believing you would not fall.

Willow, NY, August 1979

DRUNK ON A GLACIER,
TALKING TO FLIES
1980–1987

Twice-Born

In some curve of the road a car, truck, train
is waiting to stop you, gearing up even now
to intervene in your life, breaking
the boundaries of your name and face

Afterward, you are no longer the one
you called yourself before
your gaze is shuffled into another
corner, a blank wall you cannot recognize

If at that moment you resume the threads
of the old way, something inside you
dies, crying out for space

You are torn, and new, open in the face
of the turning earth and the little
burning point you stand on, and
maybe you survive

In some corner of the earth your day
is waiting, opening a wall for you,
open on the other side.

Willow, NY, May 1980

Letter to the Edge of a Field

I notice
Perseus holding the road up ahead
swallows circling their holes
at twilight
Algol under the hill

I notice (are you listening, field?)
dark spaces in the Milky Way
synchronized with bullfrog
plucked bass string
the bow at full tilt saw-toothed hum.

Lake Hill, NY, July 1980

154

Third Visit to Yeats's Grave

Clouds not moving
red eye sun sits in the water
old tower and cross stand at the highway
nothing happens
raucous wheeling crows
carry away the oak trees

ancient fire slips into and out
of every day
to go through the deaths
leave them behind you
the honest sound of a woman
at her shears at sundown

and to walk away now
to the stablest valley floor
the sun ironing the grass in place
and stand, the body
part of what it worships
wholly.

Drumcliff, Ireland, August 1980

Queen Camel's Song

Hercules the hero rides
the midheavens of northern sky
he and the snake charmer
side by side
Nameless kneeler, why do they say
you're running?

Your club flung out in the apex
of the sun's way, what is
your other hand doing?
Are your neck muscles grown
large with ritual,
your hands flung out as you pray?

Here's a card game
someone plays the crown
the poet puts her lyre down
and the plough is just a rumor
You're nearest to the serpent tamer,
kneeler, I'll raise you five

The swan flies north,
you straddle the hills with that
club in your hand
Do you run and fight at once
or are we one in this,
I mistook your stance, you
and I are simply kneeling?

Queen Camel, the "wise woman"
of Southwest England, 3500 BC,
was depicted as the main female
figure, Virgo, in the northern sky.
Hercules, also called Nameless
Kneeler, is the main male figure.
They are two of the giant earth-
works in Somerset County built to
mirror the stars. All the other
images are nearby constellations.

Rosselare-LeHavre, September 1980

156

SALUT, PARIS!

for Alex Braun

Stalking encounters of the life that was
dredging up minefields of former
innocence, *clochards* who taught
the street language
distancing in great strides of lost shelter
twice-born, listening

Receiving in great ceremony the soul
to tea, the past lives dreamy now,
visages plastered on particular
street corners, renovated bars
old friends
impregnated in cobblestones

Lament for the old childhood,
passing the street lamps of deserted square,
the answered prayers of this or that job
by the river, the stoic pose
of the shouting angel, lament the naive
rutting in fields of the clothed encounters

The angel saw a thing the saint
cannot discover
the stepladder dream over primal seas
the crashing tidal wave of stone walls
city streets Apollinaire saw once
still shuddering for the prodigal son.

Paris, September 1980

157

Sad Song Without a Name

Warm oil and a splash of cold water
come together under the covers
the smell of corn, you said,
and thousands of birds
in the collar of early morning

How do you sleep tonight
in your tender sceptical bed
your arm searching out the back of my neck
your thigh the back of my thigh?

Hunched over vigil of 3 a.m.
a cup of water without reflection
we live alone and die alone
isn't that what I said?

Virgin Mary of the kiosks
and plastic flowers
we do not make love on the marble slabs
and the crypts get smaller and smaller.

Paris-Amsterdam, September 1980

158

IN PLACE OF BONES

A barren plain
whistles through a crack in the window
in Paris, on a side street
rachitic limbs in a two-step
peruse the corners for marionettes
dim sideshows under lowering skies

The summer was spent in laughter
November broods now, taciturn
and non-committal
herons stand in gray pools, melancholy
and a little person insinuates himself
into the earlobe

Someone plays music far away
someone who has not heard of winter
who runs a threadbare tightrope
at the edge of a roof
someone cackles in a brown cafe
on a grizzly night

the one I want
to furnish with coffers
mahogany table, anarchic song.

Amsterdam, September 1980

CATSKILL DROUGHT

I wait with the rest of dense
foliage for relief
no water the body gives
replenishes roots of garden apple tree
silence stretches itself out
on the backs of crickets
no rain

the circle of hills snaps shut
wide view of distant seas
and north atlantic
boat through constellations
shed their skin

a sun I have run to
horizon to horizon stops me here
sere grass and dryer prospects
I can't remember why I came
or what my name was when I entered
where the road is that
leaves again

the bards knew best
they wept at fixed hereditary walls
sang till the cells
in the stone picked up their cry
and altered horizons

the tourniquet slips taut
the gangrenous limb falls off

imagination
drained of flight
like so many dead lawns, silent

gullies wrinkle the hills and wait
no rain.

Willow, NY, September 1980

BREAD VS. POEM

for Raymond the Cab Driver

What of the arm raised up and casting
a shadow—
is this all there is?
'That we live at last from the comb
and the stains on the handkerchief'?
César Vallejo spent his whole
adult life meticulously
guarding the wool in his trousers
durability down to a science
writing for men who need tomorrows
he wouldn't relent

You think I am fat, Raymundo?
That I have five loaves in the freezer?
All I own is what I can carry away
on my back, I know that
take away my dream
of what is beyond me, and I am nothing

If bread is only bread in the morning
and the arm raised up
is just a shadow on the wall
then kill me now
eliminate this dreamer from the ranks
I have nothing to give but sunset
that is more than sunset
nothing to give but the killer instinct

backed against the wall
if you rob me of what I am
then take the rest—

Bustelo, a loaf of bread and my
canister of sugar on a string
held out of the reach of red ants
in the desert, out of the reach of
flies of the intellect

Take it, Aristotle. In your garden
only bread grows. I can't
live on that.

NYC, December 1979

163

NIGHTCRAWLER

Plan your hesitation around the moon
stuck like the tree limbs at the bottom of the river
Gaze out the window at 3 p.m., before the light falls
shadows on the walkway are precarious
a mime engaged in skinny dances
tunnels under the eyelids, pirouettes

You have not decided where to go, the shadows
enter revolving doors, a curl in the lip
of a wave is flattened
you have not decided which door is yours
you open many, two dimensional photos, clipped
from a magazine and filed

The cards get wrinkled, none of the gestures
support the back, the surface curls up
skin of an eye, detached
reviewing parades over your shoulder
profiles rub against the wall
a patina of shoulders lurching
down the hallway

You are alone. In the basement the city
is opening for business
you hang out on the stoop and see no one
the ancestral carriage speeds by
on urgent business
deaf to departures it rides the night
midheavens, constant.

Willow, NY, November 1981

LAMMAS

Owl woman
squats at midnight
sits fullbellied on the hills
at noon

hayfields
heavy with the sun
the channels
open
to the baby grain

a pilgrimage
includes the holy body
passing
over and into the power
of fountains, tower
on a lonely hill

we have passage
to the dark field
ample foothold on the craggy
climb the body
holy animal its footsteps
plant the dark the light behind us
we are shouldering the stars.

Silbury, England, August 8, 1980

O pagan poet you
And I are one
In this—we lose our god
At set of sun.
 —Paddy Kavenaugh

OLD WOMAN OF AUTUMN

Hallowe'en night. Open the window. Listen to the footsteps
of everything out there walking. The oak leaves falling. Brooms
in all the corners, the wind is sweeping. Pilgrim footsteps
stitch the hills. Midway point in the journey to the dark.

>Stags pursue the oak leaves dreaming
>acorns in the autumn dusk
>She stands under a dry moon turning
>hills and fields to rust.

The window opens by itself. Shine on a trumpet between the
 eyes.
Lone star in insomniac forest. The rusty stream bed sings louder
than sundown in places. The wind gathers skirts of a thousand
trees, covering tracks of larger things.

>Stags pursue the oak leaves dreaming
>acorns in the autumn dusk
>She walks under a dry moon turning
>forest and stream to rust.

Midway point into the dark, the hills already humming in bass
note winter voice. The choir of lost things. Sun eaten by a
stone mouth. Heart of sun devoured for solar plexus warmth,
where the seed sleeps.

166

Stags pursue the oak leaves dreaming
acorns in the autumn dusk
She leaps under a dry moon turning
crevice and cliff to rust.

The hills roll away, the wind touching every ledge and
        rock face.
A last celebration of red leaves, fires, wrinkled faces. I lift
my skirts up, over the flames, to the dance
        of the skinny ankles.

Stags pursue the oak leaves dreaming
acorns in the autumn dusk
She dances under a dry moon turning
sun and stars to rust.

Willow, NY, Hallowe'en 1980

Candlemas (2)

Heart of winter
holy Brigit
cloud heroic stories
creaking trees on a cold night
echo in bones clearly
hollow

ritual of candles for
the year, the lengthening
hours of daylight
crack cold breathes in bones
of warning, fleece of the ewe lamb
feathers of geese

the year begins
with silence, grasses laid in
waves across the field
in waves the river freezes
windless side of the mountain
clutching snow

it may be the holes around trees
indicate
a warmth emanating from
living things
it may be
the dark calls the sun

beeches rustle
the twins and hunter stand crystalline

168

at dark, all legends of the bear
are true
we cannot see
it may be the hill are singing.

Willow, NY, February 2, 1981

BELTANE

Hay fires roll down dragon hill
the strolling planets in
single file
stars above us, stars below us
three times around the pillar of stone
three times around the well
we follow the sun

Thrust of peas, garlic, onion grass
old iron in the fields bereft
stone ardor of buried cold
in the spears of crocus, iris, daffodil
the arching foot of jonquil
at attention

Battered coat of ravenous deer
cropping bright green grasses
the white-tailed rabbit leaps
four feet in the air
trillium opens at the mouth of a cave
by the fiddle bow, wild onion

Mating woodpeckers hammer on
live trees, loud, insistent
crones wait for warm hands, watching
as the plow goes in
you are old, old
the king and the queen meet
once again.

Willow, NY, May 1, 1982

170

LURIGANCHO

for Juan Cuadros

A solitary air blows over the cerro
the sun, disguised in the white
soup of Lima, is vaguely waving

Guards with official whistles
harry the listener
calling each other through corridors
they shriek and answer
shriek and answer
barking dogs at midnight
in a little town—
the visits are over

Brick walls, broken windows
inmates in brightly colored shirts
are waving
the only flower in the grainy air
the only color

Holes are broken through brick walls
into cubicles
to search outsiders
the left arms of women tattooed
with numbers
the personal shakedown
the last touch across the crotch
to prove we are women

Outside the walls machine guns
strut through abandoned market days
leering into the hurried business
of thousands of women
struggling into lines for the buses
exchanging news and embraces
to last the week
the men at the windows are waving
waving

Saludos, hermanos
where we know each other
there are no walls
no twisted dreams of day after day
but a clear wind over the Andes
the gentle touch of *garúa* moistening
hands and hair

Ciao, South American continent
the murders in your face
are less disguised than where I live—
one sees who to hate
To the north the civilized killers
corporate fists, the ones in power
have no human face at all.
They have no face.

Lurigancho, Lima, Perú, September 1982

SONG FOR 5 A.M.

We arm ourselves
the deaf soldier with his shield
we take great care with the latest
disguise

slippery fish
swim against the rocks
you can't catch them
we can't
sliding faces turn the corner
you can't, I can't
nobody can

Ourselves surprised.
Vaguely reminiscent of a fall rain
anguish drops
the bodies naked
a rest in love
like the beggar's portrait
immune to tuberculosis

There is a power in leaves
the separate names of everyone
in the forest
the leaves change
we change
there is a power.

Willow, NY, September 1982

173

CALL IT WINDOW

for Chuck & Dustin

That crash in the rainy night
was no animal
a tree fell, down by the stream
the fog bank carries the air in
green sprouts, dank earth
dark clothes
every insect alive on the hillside
visits this lamp.

Willow, NY, June 1983

174

For the Audience

of the Living Theater

At ease then in your shell
the simple waters
break/confine
the night, not

something to recline in
restlessness
concedes to terror
former prerogatives gone

the only safety is a middle ground
between self and
the other, between action
and nothing at all

Lavender awnings mask
a quiet face
a quiet night in
the jungle

owls on separate branches
sing of death
the little selves staked out
like decoys

If it turned out to be not
a playpen

or protected environment,
drugs ticked off the fingers

if it turned out to be
an experiment in valor
not what you could
but were bound to do
and every step bore along its cost
and accusation

And if there were a censor
stopping you at the turnpike gate
asking

What have you taken, what have you given
tonight?

What then?

NYC, January 1984

176

Visiting Hours

for Asher Rosen

The cornerstone of the hospital
cuts the sky, a white sky
it will snow tonight
people are dashing across the street
you are not in a rush
nor am I

In the clutter of ashtrays
a table sits in a corner
with two people at it, you and me
obliterating the silence of poets
by talking talking over the table
into the streets

Your right hand is trembling
from your laughter
it is difficult to discern
your age
your radical stance intact
after eighty years

The cornerstone cuts the air
someone cut your eyebrows, their
bristling extravagance curtailed
you frown, you on your side
of those eyelids, me on the other
we are not in a rush

In the hospital corner I hold
your hand, ruminating
on the cramped spaces we create
and the amplitude of the soul that will
brook no closets
bedchambers, mourning gowns

My friend, without your eyebrows
or your teeth
without your laughter
the soul not always attached to the body
the one thing we have no use for
is a closet

Stand back! I want to shout
at the doctors. Give this man some room!
He is a poet.

St. Vincent's Hospital, NYC,
December 1983–February 1984

Past Time

Southwest wind comes
the knees collapse, the apron, skirt,
the knees collapse
I wish you would've been home tonight
I think of you still

the southwest wind comes
sultry over the river
fog
I went to see you and you had
already gone

I picture you with a lover
you
a nomad finding his hearth
in giving
the delicate act of giving

the southwest wind comes
bigger than you or me
the river breaks
and flows
the wind blows over and over

there is nothing to say

Woodstock, NY, February 1985

LILITH

for Joe Trusso

Lilith the equal
walked the earth
she came in her southwest wind
her sultry
forest on the landscape

she came with hair
short
sticking out at angles
and her prowess, the lion's mane
walked into the water

she said, you address
my knees
the entity of my knees
and I rise
rise

I have witnessed every game
unconquered
I give what I choose, no one
but an equal
can take from me

I am the southwest wind
my breasts lean into the water
my neck devours the actual stars

my mind cranes into a precipice
where darkness and I are one

who
sang the owl woman
who can play and laugh
and love and kill
like me?

only one
who salutes my freedom
and power, and smiles
for a moment
into my dark eyes.

Woodstock, NY, Spring 1985

THERE WAS A WOMAN

for Betty MacDonald

After wringing the guts out
ricocheting in a small room
off corners, solitudes, blind surfaces,
bird flapping at the wings of her cage
animal in the hills at twilight
turning round and round
the tense enclosure
somersaulting in the dark

there was a woman
she lived, and she died
there was a woman
she lived, and she died
there was a woman
she lived, and while she lived
she sang

What catches them there?
Meridel's arms across the prairie
Alice Walker's world in her eye
Amadeus in his anthems
Raymond Chandler's letters at dawn
What keeps them
working it out on the threshing floor
waiting for the one swift flight
the one swift flight when the bird
soundless
leaves the horizon empty

182

there was a woman
she lived, and she died
there was a woman
she lived, and she died
there was a woman
she lived, and while she lived
she sang

Contemplating the final version
spread out on the rug
in the interstices of window/stream
dichotomy, one half of you
holds on, the other half is
running down the hill
and while you wait with the final chorus
you have already gone

there was a woman
she lived, and she died
there was a woman
she lived, and she died
there was a woman
she lived, and while she lived

she reconciled earth to branches
ear to the ground
reconciled the chorus of tree frogs
and the one singing in her head

there was a woman
she lived, and while she lived
she sang.

Woodstock, NY, April 1985

183

Human Prayer

Sing Sing entrance
stands over the shore line
of the Hudson River

to the left
behind barbed wire topped wall
is a ball field
someone hits a triple as the sun
goes down

to the right
sprawled along the river
is lover's lane, a kid
peels out in a blue car,
the squeal of tires

and one side is inside
and one side is outside
the same plane passing through
the same sky over both

inside, walking out
through stone corridors
I rub a little lipstick on the wall.

Sing Sing, Ossining, NY, June 1985

The Ancient Waltz

Ancient page in the history book
of a civilized world
the band at the all night tavern
plays another chorus
the drummer with impeccable teeth
studies his woman among the dancers,
smiles

purple and maroon trumpets play
till dawn
a music of old people
sighs from the furniture on the balcony
address the night
the woman watches her lover's arms
beating down the fog

trumpets flash brass and copper
winking at the old people going down
maroon corridors
where the sea
and its inevitable gravity
absorb the night

stained glass masks the vulnerable
faces falling
helplessly in love
the woman watches her drummer
his hands falling
tac tac tac
while the singer in enormous jacket
serves up a bolero

Viva la historia!
shouts a voice from the tables
the page now crowded with day after day
turns brown, becomes another page,
is discovered in the desert of
extra-terrestrial airports
where the writing, indecipherable,
smells of hot sauce.

Barranco, Lima, Perú, September 1985

PASTO RURI

Where are you going
sister fly?
Don't get lost in that
footprint
I'd say
lend me your wings
but you can't
How would you reach
Jiri Shanka?

You know and I know
the glacial moraine
and the earth down there
is not my hat
nor the brim of my hat
My heart is beating
so hard
I can't
tell them apart

Where are you going
sister fly?
Don't get lost in that
footprint
I'd say
lend me your wings
but you can't
How would you reach
Jiri Shanka?

Pasto Ruri, 15,500 ft. glacier

Jiri Shanka, facing peak,
approximately 16,500 ft.

Huaraz, Perú, September 1985

187

Room on the Third Floor

What can I say to your sleeping back?
Thoughts won't reach the color
of your shirt, or the angel
over your face
and the parrot on my tongue
doesn't jump tonight

your dreams of dying alone
and abandoned
a stone buried in the earth
like any other
how did we get to this quiet sheet
stretched out over the blood of trees
cut down on street corners?

my impatience
at having no fixed place
at never being satisfied
and your calm in the face of my
absolute and interminable resistance,
how is it we found each other, drawn in
by mouths of different legends
laughter spelled out in separate tongues?

Cantínflas jumps on the rickety catwalk
day after day he runs without falling
and the heart of a poet reels drunkenly
on a glacier, talking to flies

the buried stone has become a flower
and in its voice
the wind sings, a bird is flying.

Miraflores, Lima, Perú, September 1985

Balcony Door

Like the dumb beasts going
down to the river
I follow you step by step
and unaccustomed now to solitude
seek out every friend
only in the creases of sleep appear
sporadically the stars at night, a clear
night, and the soul unafraid

my friends came to me in sleep
my women friends, wearing wigs and
laughing
the man I danced with was a monster
he had no neck, he was built like a wall
a solid wall against which one would writhe
and my women friends were waiting
for me, laughing

my hands find no place to spread
themselves out, to declare themselves
on the table
I clasp them between my legs and bow
my head, I am unhappy without you
my glasses reflect the door behind me
open, contradicting the victim
as a normal condition

I am perfectly content, staring at
the yellow flowers on the bedspread,
to graze on the sunny porches

but I am tied and gagged
You know the soft
purring animal, the sounds of night
but the fire that lights up my
skull is a stranger.

Miraflores, Lima, Perú, September 1985

AMERICAN ARTISTS

My friends and I sat on the
picnic table
we talked about how the world was
how we wanted it to be
the table was slanted
we ate our lunch
a cold air running through our fingers

Who knows about the farms inside
the ones we carry around
—if the crops are gathered
or the well is dry
or the roots
wrenched out of the earth?
we sat together and ate our lunch

Half revealed in the gray light
were the stones of ourselves, our bones
and molars, none of us were fat
nor clearly defined
lines wavered about the chin as the roads
composed themselves
and the landscapes settled

An element of fear sat in the scarred
photographs, the torn posters
and revelatory dreams
a complicity of misery in the gnarled
hands of sharecroppers, migrant workers

exiles born out of a country
no one saw any more

Then, like a wind buried in the tree line
that comes singing over the heads
of the farmers a forgotten tune
someone laughed
we all laughed
we jumped up and down on the table
the farms followed us home.

Willow, NY, October 1985

THE WALK

A woman, twisted at the edge of her seat,
walks into the woods
walks blindly, she intends to scream
she intends to walk to the old friend,
the hickory tree at the top of the road,
and fling her arms around him, and pound
the snow at his feet.

Instead, she walks a little farther.
She doesn't want the light across the meadow
in on her screams; the family in there, blanking
out the sound during commercials, alerted unexpectedly
to the wild dreams of trees.
She continues climbing, past the maple tree of a hundred
walks, her feet striding purposefully
into the dark.

The stars come suddenly to her, decorating
the arms of the forest—Orion, Sirius, Pleiades,
Hyades, Auriga, Perseus
and Algol the demon star thrust out from him
due north Polaris over the hill
And she doesn't want to build another bookshelf
She doesn't want to pocket this away,
to squirrel it into some quiet corner where
she will never find it again.

She reaches the stream. It is the only darkness
in the forest, and the only time she takes out
her flashlight. Where she was stepping was indeed

194

a rock. What she reached for was the water.
Her hands are warm. It is an old pact
between her and the beech trees rustling on the path.
Her war is with herself, herself and containment
not against the footsteps of a path, or the sensible
way out, but against the ironing out of wildness,
her own wildness.

Her heart is stirred as a creature under trees
looking up at lights. No wind, the tears roll down
her face. She is safe in her love for the stars,
the water, her commitment to beauty.
Is it beauty, really? Does it matter?
She doesn't build shelves, nor bookcases,
with every book a brick one keeps for safety
hidden in the corner. Her love turns a corner,
it dips over the rise in the hill, and whoops down
the other side. Perhaps her books will be kisses,
wet leaves under the snow that show up dark
on a moonless night.

Perhaps she will never reach Jerusalem on a camel,
or see the Southern Cross again. The north woods
is where she happens to be, divining the branches
before they hit her face. Perhaps she will never
build a bookcase. Perhaps she doesn't have to.

Willow, NY, January 1986

LITTLE GHOST IN THE STATION

for Richard Manuel

Looking through the window down the track
to the north, she peeled a piece of plastic
from the pane
the birds would have a hard time of it
tonight, the frozen wind, the waves
looping and crashing on the rocks,
especially the migratory birds,
the white-throated sparrow who had just
appeared in the courtyard yesterday
and sung his heart out

The plastic scraping rose in the draft
from the track below
and she thought of her mother
who thought of the birds
on the fiercest mornings, and threw
them bread with bacon drippings
The plastic fluttered up again
a tiny dybbuk in the window corner,
a tiny message from her mother,
a voice on the phone from far away

She worried about the birds, too
especially that one, God's flute player
who gave her spring at the fire escape
when she whistled and he answered
the same four notes he sang in the Catskill

summers when she reached a peak
"Poor John is dead," he sang,
and now it was winter, quiet at the window,
and she did not need a cigarette
she needed to weep.

Ossining, NY, February 1986

MR. PLANT, A PORTRAIT

for Chuck Culhane

A goat jumps over a pile of leaves,
a green plant, to be specific,
and it's Tuesday
he jumps through the door wearing
sneakers, humming to himself

It's a large square room we have
for the workshop, outside are
the armed guards
on the windows, bars
and in this room a freedom that
like some champagnes
doesn't travel

Mr. Plant's in a chipper mood
slinging around *damp cap*
two sounds he likes, until he
fits them perfectly into the picture
of a wall, a damp wall, and an army
marching foolishly down the track

On that blue/red star he calls
home his laugh is easy
his biggest jokes reserved
for himself, the human bean, silliest
of God's creatures

The sun goes down over the Palisades
across the river brilliant bands
of gold serenade the eye
from the blue/red star the plant
looks out the window.

Willow, NY, April 1986

SKYWRITING

for Ramón

The sky tonight is crimson and green
crimson and green
like Munch's ecstatic painting of the woman
in the grove at sundown suddenly quiet
enjoying herself
you can see the clouds wave good-bye
to the mountains as they tiptoe off
the letters there might almost be Hebrew
in silky pastels

There is a country, I keep
telling myself
where the messages are writ so large
even the impassioned blind can see them
then again, maybe not
just because fields are ready for
planting doesn't mean
the corn's already down there, green and
waiting, or that raccoons will scream
at night, their hands heavy with plunder

might, might not be
might, might not, the chattering crows
wheel off
a strict translation of the solemn
raucous company of thieves.

Woodstock, NY, April 1986

200

THE FLOOD

Archangel Mary falls into the water
killing the bridges, the Tappan Zee
and railroad trestles. Her backside against
the pier, they promenade
across her, River Edge to Harlem,
and time runs out

Archangel Mary, dressed as a chorus girl
waits by Big Ben in the harbor
It's not midnight yet, she stands
in the cascades covering her face,
kicks out from the deluge in Paris
and dreams in bed

He watches her through the bars
he thinks she's trapped
She is sleeping
flood waters rise
She is safe and smiling
caught in a dream of sunlight
shining on the coins around her face

Out of the Bedouin desert her ankle
steps into a taxi in London
Someone offers her a ring, the coins
hide her face
She is safe and smiling, playing the piano
in an unguarded moment, water pours through
her window to the street

He has come down from the rooftop
in a suit of chimneys
In her private ocean Archangel Mary
watches him sail by the quay
she lights a candle in the mirror
she likes his face.

Sing Sing, Ossining, NY, May 1987

LIMA IN WINTER

Without sun the edges blur between dream
and reality, crowds of people hurry along
in the mist without umbrellas
It is night. You vaguely see their outlines
against the headlights.

The people are planting flowers,
acres of yellow flowers, as a symbol of life
after death, the death of a government,
Chile specifically. They are eating the flowers,
roots and stems, to harbor the joy inside.

On a damp street corner a menacing youth
asks where you are going. You are going nowhere
but his posture coming toward you
makes you grab the first bus you see.
In the house are two women, you and another,
dressed in fantastically ornate gowns
that somewhat match, you decide,
and fit the occasion.

She snaps your picture, looking unusually well
and sexy, you can't wait to show it to your lover
He is there, suddenly, you would follow him
anywhere. A long kiss, rising desire, and
you step back: he's a short fat man
with an affable face.

And the statue of the pregnant Virgin?
he asks. Wasn't she standing here?
Your memory doesn't stretch back that far.
She's in the kitchen, you say, between candles.
He smiles. I thought maybe she had her baby.

You keep going at midnight to the sordid clinics
to get another shot on the right.
People line up to watch, and you come out rubbing
your cheek, feeling curiously sexual.
The intern claims he has hands of gold
and refuses to charge you.

The lines are blurred. Two people are sleeping
on the narrow bed, chest to back, knees inside
knees, one's arms wrapped around the other.
They dream of sleeping chest to back,
their knees inside knees, their dreams
interchanging as they turn in bed.

The price of cough drops depends
on what you are wearing, what time it is,
the poverty of the vendor, and the street corner.
Tanks pass bristling with rifles, everybody
looks the other way. They talk of stolen
earrings, and the sadness of winter.

A crowd on the corner is anxiously watching
a red gym bag next to the lamp post.
It could be a bomb, a baby, a cocaine drop,
or somebody's gym bag, forgotten when
he crossed the street. They keep on watching.

The lines lead to perplexity. The body revolts
against cigarettes, and keeps on smoking.
Inside the gray palace the plants bloom
brilliantly. They could almost be yellow.
We have started to eat.

Lima, Perú, August 1986

For the Master Singer

for Laurent

The elements separate, Johann Sebastian
and I run to the cliffs with small steps
drinking in

sea sky water mist
and sweat on the shoulders

the elements separate, Johann Sebastian
and falling on one's knees
is not enough

no, not enough in the times we live in
light clothes, walking shoes
like the poets of our days
wandering through catacombs,
cathedrals, certain of echoes
directing us

to go out at midnight
Johann
is not enough

We need, despite the tenderness of earth
for our bodies
lavender wind, translucent air
that plucks the feathers of our drunken
crewcut and leaves us helplessly exposed
the flame headed child

I have also lapped at the bowl
of the all forgiving
much work to be done, sang the waves
I could hardly contain myself
the baptismal font ran red
with desire
the young man and I leaned languidly
over, convinced it was blood

What never changes, Johann
is desire
sweet desire
knows its name is written on doors
and runs eagerly to find
what church what well
what holy font will give me?

Give me, sings desire
sweet desire
give me or I'll die
knees skin and eyes sing
take me
sensate elemental mother
take me, here I am.

Lima, Perú, August 1986

207

ATALAYA

for Daniel Pinto Rey

Arch of the foot
over the stones from the river
arch of the foot
over the round stones from the river
on the road of dust and stones
it's one o'clock
jungle time, and there's no way out
no flights, no boats, the sun
a grill on the tin roofs

From the warm bench
the clouds,
realities inside other realities,
surfaces turning over while we sleep
and time stops
enormously slow time cranks to a halt
and our feet seek out the stones
the stones from the river

Enchantment sits in the trees
in the growing bush and the cries of the cock
her fingers reach out from the branches
of the mamei in the plaza
of the mango and the cashew
the little clothes, hanging from hooks
in the market, rock in the wind

Time stopped, the wind sweeps the plaza
and the slow rolling laugh of the mother
under the river moves the stones
there is no way out
no place other than here
no time other than now
the slow beating of the heart

A curious tenderness in the perimeters
of the web she weaves
all her children are happy
nailed to the wall
the women, like trees walking, are all satisfied
with the proud eyes of savage birds
they watch the river

The wind over the plaza brings the news
we've already heard more than once
no planes come in, no planes go out
no canoes, no boats
time stops
there is no way out of the jungle today.

Atalaya, Perú, August 1986

MADRE SELVA

Madre Ayahuasca
we sit in a circle in the dark
and wait for your voice
we come out of separate starlit chambers
like animals into the courtyard
to smoke mapacho and wait
for your voice

Cocodrilo cocodrilo sings the night bird
called Maria
Mariiia Mariiia sings the crocodile
We listen for your footsteps
lit with the comic presence of your
headlights beaming in colored arches,
a magic tree that obscures your face

In the name of the Señora
sings Don Domingo
in the room of night he seeks us out
we ourselves are the meal in her honor
here on this river where she is loved
on this continent where she is worshiped
the dark
smiles in us with radiant teeth

Standing inside our dreams the curandero
is everywhere among us, we cannot
see his face, his bouquet of sweet basil
shakes away danger, his tapestry waves away
invalid spirits, the smoke he blows

in our hair cures night blindness
the young boy sees the snakes approaching
and doesn't scream

Madre Selva Cosmic Mother
here we are peeled open
waiting.

Urubamba river, Ucayali province, Perú,
September 1986

Roses in the Throat

Dust on the plastic roses
in the restaurant
red dirt jungle town
and one by one they die
the splendid dreams, impossible
sunsets on the lake
picture post cards of an ideal world
falling
dust by dust on the windows

There is no full moon
the day of possibilities was yesterday
and we already woke up
with dust in our throat from old philosophies
dust of the orator at his pulpit
who puts us to sleep
history lessons of somnolent
high school teachers
empty words
hawking their tickets home in the town square
and nobody buying

Dust on the roses
and the perfect profile
of an angel
tranquilly reading her comic book
and eating, unaware
of her mouth, her eyes, her rosy power

Dust on the roses
and the canker sore of the intellect
thrust into a paradise it can
never comprehend
capturing in its vigil
sides of faces, profiles, living legends
socking them away for another time

invisible without a face
when the heart will sing
and sing
and animate the stories
born full-bodied from the chest
so there is no room for dust
or plastic roses

Impossible then to create
in the fullness of life?
Impossible to give birth to a story,
a poem, *and* a child of the body?
The dust on the roses lies mute
immobile
the song is half lament
half lullaby
an owl calls from across the river
half lullaby half lament.

Pucallpa, Perú, September 1986

GRANDMOTHER

for Harry B.

The mountain won me
she took me over her back and won me
lying down on the path at dusk
I looked up into her trees
swirling
stark antennas
muscular beeches holding their leaves

November light on her orange fur
of ferns, blasted already by frost
and wind
the oval vaginas in boulders carved
by ice wind and water
birthday cake tiers nearing the top
the mountain won me

stretched me out
and whistled along old electric lines
she sent one bird as messenger
from tier to tier
as I came down, a small white bird
surprised at footsteps chomping down
the distance in cold November

wan light white bird
face upraised into snow flurries
distant valleys mottled

with sunlight
mauve and russet coat of fallen leaves

bleached ivory grasses
and fat corkscrewed torsos of birches
fighting for their edge
she won me heart hoof and eye
leaping down the stream bed

she let me lie there
under the swirling branches
under the snow
invited me to lie down
in the middle of the road
just as I wanted

she carried me on her back
like some marsupials
until I was old enough
to watch which way the stars fell
and open the holes they left
in the inner eye.

Graham Mountain, NY, November 1986

215

Greeting Card

In the meridian of early morning
beset by merchants of romance
remember,
widdershins of the dance floor,
total recall resides
in the small pulse at the wrist,
the small steps into the amphitheater
taken

Drive me over the rapids of any
foreign river, watch if I remember
how to swim

Yes I do. So do you.
Happy New Year.

Woodstock, NY, December 31, 1986

LETTER FROM THE WOODS

It's eight o'clock, the birds are calling—
the hermit thrush,
the wood thrush, the preacher bird,
and the conversationalist
whose real name I wish I knew
Crow passes, the light gets darker
and I'm resting here for five minutes
thinking of you

I ate my way up the side of the mountain
grazed at the top
and ate my way down
Bright yellow green on stone outcroppings
mauve and deep purple in the groves
I've been thinking of you
and addressing the trees, hugging the old ones,
all day thinking

Turkey buzzard has a tiny red head
he flew by the summit
while we ate, and a top-heavy grouse
dived off into the woods
What did you do all day
under the sky?
One butterfly had an iridescent body
with a double set of purple wings.

Windham High Peak, NY, July 6, 1987

217

SLIDE

There is nothing like my dream
In my heart I offer a white
chrysanthemum
to Dorothy in a giant's dress,
Kuan Yin's swan in the winter hills

One end of the mountain trail is blue,
the other pink
like two eyes discovered in infancy
at the curtain stretchers in family home,
one eye sees blue, the other pink

The trail below the sun line flanked
with crystal trees
a thousand shades of blue white
tunnel upward
and the ridge line, afternoon sun
through prisms, golden pink hosannas,
there is nothing like my dream

No sound. One grouse flushed out
from the underbrush. No tracks.
No wind.
   The hills below the white world
gold and nowhere private.
Green ice walls, like the teeth
in glacial fissures,
     birch catkins
in the broken snow, there is
nothing like my dream.

Slide Mountain, NY, December 31, 1986

218

Return to Sender / Inmate Is Dead

for Hector Algarín

Dear Hector:
This is how my letter came back
and the job does not get easier
Our casualties behind the walls are buried
with numbers instead of names,
numbers that have nothing to do with birthdays,
dreams, or completed works.
What are the odds we can make
a dent in the system?

I want everyone in this country
to stop that train, says Brian Wilson,
Viet Nam vet peace activist.
I'm driving down Interstate 90, holding
your letter in my lap while he lies
on the tracks. And gone! His legs are gone!
Mowed down by munitions train bound with bombs
for Nicaragua. What are the odds
we dent in a cast-iron system?

I'm pulling out every Sing Sing folder
looking for you—your poems, your letters,
your voice on the Christmas tape
over and over
Jigsaw pieces. The person I know caught
in glimpses, like the mirror you
spoke into at the Christmas reading.

In a room with too many lights on
a paper clip dropped in a stone bowl
makes three syllables—a tiny sound—
and I know the mortality I carry
in my breastbone, the tilt of my shoulders.
The river, swollen with rain, is roaring

RETURN TO RETURNER / INMATE IS NOT DEAD
Inmate is not inmate.
Bucephalus whinnies into starry space.
The blood under the bridge is the bridge.
The miracle is a green face of freedom.
No them. Just all of us.

Willow, NY, September 1987

220

AMERICAN WALLS
1988–1999

For all the people I have worked and shared
and written with inside American prisons

MUSHROOM

for Chuck, Sal, Armando, Gary, Ringo, Marty,
Odette, Babe, Jack, Traci, Hank, Dougie,
Hector, Milton, Kip, Jackie, Beekie, Sonya,
Pumpkin, Michele, Crystal, Yasin, Donna, and
all the others behind bars

When I woke up this morning, I saw it clearly:
cancer pressing in at the windows
like a pale fluffy mushroom
growing on the bars
of all the jails and prisons of America
waiting in a pool at the exit
to attach itself to your feet
just as you leave

Fighting heroically in iron forests
we write poems, gather together
we light little candles
and congratulate ourselves on small successes
another voice in the chorus, another
consciousness in the web and fabric of us
clandestinely fighting back,
and then you leave

Outside the forest of iron trees
and visible campfire, you hit the street
and the same conditions that ever propelled
you to rebellion, anger, self-destruction
slam you in the face

Mushroom has already caught onto the lip
of your sole, pretending to be a shadow,
and like a pale fat man with dainty fingers
starts delicately to eat

You say, *No, I didn't get high tonight!*
and, *Hey, your money is safe with me!*
Monday I'll be starting a new job.
Tomorrow I'll be down at Welfare,
Don't worry about it, sugar,
it's only wine.
Lend me thirty dollars till Tuesday,
I'll pay you back.

And all the shadows we fought together
huddled around the light
together
naming and condemning the enemy
all the shadows we extirpate with song
rise up, they take up lodgings again
in you, in me
It's no big secret, we carry the spores
around in the soles of our feet.

D Train, NYC, February 1991

In the Nick of Winter Time

A handful of sand on the slope
and the tires have traction
one bag of sand in back of the car
two bags over the wheel wells
the car digs in
and fishtails up the mountain

Four pieces of firewood
keep the tarp stapled to dry ground
ready for the next cord
one fifty dollar bill in the visor
of the plow man's truck keeps the road clear
and the next cord lumbering uphill

One lightbulb
under the lid of the water house
where the pipe comes from the spring
out of the ground, and stands
vulnerable and brittle in the sub-zero night
one lightbulb is all that stands between
running water and frozen pipes

the lit bulb bright as a new penny
through the peephole near the bathroom floor
the final checkpoint before going to bed
one planet on the western horizon
joined by another, less brilliant
in the full moon blue snow night

one armload of kindling

cut from the white birch blowdown
half a tree makes one rack of kindling
waiting at the stove door for removal of ashes
so the dance can begin
no detail overlooked or forgotten, as though
the world hung in the balance

a thick black rag at the doorsill, the shovel
in bucket of sand on the porch
the wood stacked according to dryness
kitty litter dumped on icy curves up the driveway
the barrels en route filled with sand and salt
and every nook and cranny of the roadbed
checked to ensure safe passage

this is the temperature to make oatmeal cookies
into exact configurations of nuts and raisins
ginger, cinnamon, and nutmeg
this is the time to polish the hearth
light candles to the Goddess without a face
fill the woodbox, sit in the draft free
nook, ruminate and read

I was definitely born by a winter fire
and a sun at low angle in the sky
even in sleep my instincts
find the clear reflection in a bus window
I turn my face toward the azimuth
like a key in my forehead
as though the angle itself were enough
to nose forward, eyes closed, to the light.

Willow, New York, January 1996

226

your blues

for Paul Butterfield

dear butter
your blues
your mouth harp sweet
chicago
winter nights
the club is packed, your band
is hot, the building
gets up by itself
boogies down to bearsville
and if you ain't doin' it still,
who will?
dear butter, your sweet
translation of the solemn
into raunchy strut
and get up
wrong side of the bed again
your blues

Woodstock, NY, July 1987

227

TREK

Moose woman antler man
traces of porcupine over the snow
through deer hobble bushes
winter sun
bigger than summer sun
clearer cold translucent

Antler man moose woman
snowshoes tracking up the ravine
she almost beat me, that grim visage
not so kind to someone outside her cave
not so kind the green woman
so exacting

She almost beat me down
my heart stopped, rattled
I stopped, blood evacuating legs
and brain stem. Why go on?
What great merciful face
is my companion?

Merciful face my own blamelessness
no guilt no judge
no jury of my peers
What color is the sky?
Not guilty.

The knowledge that I will die right here
becomes possible error
I could run down, give it up

I could hike out
the summit is too close to turn back

Moose woman antler man
hand signals drew in the hierophants
on the street, it was
years ago, but the city was mostly
empty, the initiates few

So I've come back
balanced on the edge, to make
mudras of compassion, ask for
more rice grains, more mashed potatoes
more Elmer's Glue

because I'm out here in the soup
because I choose to.

Hunter Mountain, NY, January 1988

Greeting the Year 2000, with Respect

Glancing back at the millennium we are leaving,
I see a cannon roll out into the dust
of a tiny war in the patch of sun
in a store window
on the Lower East Side
Noise, blood, suffering, even the animals
take part; no one is winning

Great theaters of carnage
bright science yoked to bleak
military arsenals, kids are killing kids
people are torn between nationalism
and compassion, the entire human species
is hurling itself headlong off the edge.

And he laid hold on the dragon, the old serpent,
and bound her for a thousand years
and cast her into the abyss
and shut it and sealed it over her
that she should deceive the nations no more
until the thousand years be finished;
after this she must be loosed a little while.   (*Revelations 20: 2–4.*)

She must be loosed a little while?
How little a while?
Lording it over the beasts in the field,
the trees in the forest, the air, the water,
with the rapt egocentric stance that nature
is the devil, we have been supremely free
to disrespect whomever we choose.

230

I think of the lovely Lilith,
tossing her hair as she leaves the abyss
the unbound fire in every atom
She steps out into a vacant lot
in the Southeast Bronx, where to *dis*
somebody is to face down a handgun

A serpent curls among the streets
of the world, a naked energy
climbs our spine and gazes from our eyes
Don't cut the trees, don't blaze more trails
across the mountains, leave a little
wildness for the next inheritors,
with respect.

Monte Alban for a thousand years
was a sacred city and civilization
of peace. With plentiful fields
of corn, the people were free
to adorn their temple
In synchronicity with the earth
they derived their names from what they did.

Let us go out and greet the new
century, said Seraphita, Balzac's angel,
and the icy fjords cracked and melted
the bells rang wildly
With great respect, with great love
she said, and the energy
crackled across the sky like lightning.

Look at the serpent
curling through the green woods
spiralling up the hills from the flat land,
Greet the new millennium with complicity

for the unchained nature in the earth,
the air, the water,
the snake undulating up our spines
and the dragon in the stars.

Willow, NY, January 1, 1994

Morning

A mountain chain of clouds
substantial, thick
suddenly broken through by the sun

in just the way
the ego is broken through
by climbing

real mountains in a real somewhere
and you have done that
you have given me back my joy.

New York Thruway, February 1997

M42

M42
the 42nd interruption
in Charles Messier's quest for comets
the 42nd suspect on the list
the 42nd blotch and *poseur*
is not a shooting star
is not a star
What is it?

M42 in Orion's sword
is a scintillating branch
the fish mouth of the Great Nebula
the next spiral arm out from us in the galaxy
the seamless coat of Christ
a stellar swan
The pulsating blue Trapezium
is a *cuna*, a cradle giving birth
to star after star after star

From the Chinese enamel lamp
a gorgeous goose flew off
through a hole in the beaded curtain
to the recesses of stellar space
she was laughing to herself, she was shaking
with mirth, her flight described an arc
of maybe twenty-five light years
across, from wing to wing

Her laughter flew
uncontrolled from the throats

of the ancient queens
as they swigged another ale down
broke another neckbone
and threw it to the dogs

She laughed in the midnight graveyards
with adept yoginis, who sang to each other
in secret
surrounded by bones jutting through
the earth and the grinning skulls
they reeled in ecstasy

O dazzling fecund nebula
in your blue and white robe!

If you want to be present at creation
see the Goddess in Her radiant dress
the Shakti!
the Shekkinah!
Get a telescope
buy binoculars
point it at the cloud in Orion's sword,
galactic pulse of the universe,
Look at this!

The bird flying off into starry space
Look at this.

Willow, New York, November 11, 1994

MAD DOGS OF TRIESTE

for Andy Clausen

We have never been in a war like this
in all the years of watching
the street at 3 a.m.,
kids lobbing cherry bombs into garbage cans
the last hookers heading toward home

It used to be, stopping in Les Halles cafes
after a night we could find the strong
men from the market
and the beautiful prostitutes
resting in each other's arms
Le Chat Qui Peche, Le Chien Qui Fume
alive with Parisian waltzes, his hands on her ass
We could pick up raw produce from discard bins
and have lentil stew for tomorrow

Things have never been like this.
Cops square off against teenagers in the village square
take the most pliant as lovers, and reroute the rest
into chutes of incarceration
The mad dogs of Trieste
we counted on to bring down the dead
and rotting status quo, give a shove here
and there, marauder the fattened and calcified order,
have faded like stories

We used to catch them with their hat brims

236

keeping most of the face in shadow
and sometimes those voices
one by one
turned into waves
like cicadas in the August trees, whistling
receding, and the words crept under
the curtains of power, made little changes,
tilted precarious balance, and brought relief

Those packs don't crisscross the boulevards
now in the ancient cities, no political cabal
behind us watches the world with
eyes entirely
cognizant
the lyrical voices rainbow bodies
your friends my friends nobody left
but the mad dogs of Trieste as we
cover the streets.

Willow, NY, August 1998

WORD UP

for the women in Bayview C.F.

We write in gelatin
trembling at the train station
like the woman in bangles
waving out the window to her lover
down the track

and the content of what we say
is a child's cradle
where reveille is never called
and the sirens, sending best regards,
are silent

The Swiss have a word for it:
bright seal,
and *entrance denied*
Pour the light from one bowl to another
catch it in a saucer as it falls.

Bayview C.F., NYC, June 1990

To You on the Other Side of This

You cannot take away this morning
        of lilacs, the soft air in the willow tree
and his life again in the little backyard
        with his red wooden truck, playing
        until it was time for our snack and his packet
        of M&Ms until lunch.
You can't take away the eager teenager
        bounding down the steps and out to his friends
or his messy room with the socks strewn everywhere
        and the drum set awaiting his return
his love of music and magic, the card tricks and rubber
        wolf mask, his practice pad alive with
        riffs and paradiddles,
the wide excited smile of him sharing the bill with
        Tito Puente at the Union City dive.

Your stupid fear, shooting at an interloper in your
        ill-timed gas station stick-up, with your gun exposed
as though you'd been caught *ex coitus* in a phone booth
        with your pants down and your eyes still glazed.
The horrible purple flower at his neck, where the blood
        flowed: killed on contact.
And you're lucky you did not meet me then
        the wild grief in me would've torn you, tall as you are
        and strong, limb from limb
I would've knocked you to the ground and choked the life
        from you, taken it from you like you did from him
You're lucky you did not find me, trembling
        with hate and retribution.

Months passed. You have taken away
        his forward momentum, but not himself
his spirit still alive in the midst of my grieving.
You crossed over into the mystery of someone else's life
        stopped by your hands
And no one will join you in the ring as you wrestle
        with that.

They asked if I want the death penalty.
Will it bring my son back?
Let nothing cushion the truth, I say,
        of having flung up into the face of the sky
        his precious life, as though it were an afterthought
Let nothing stop the growth of consciousness
        in you, I say, until you reach the place of owning
        what you did, and feel the relentless weight of it
        on your soul, like an iron anvil.
Killing you will stop all that. It will make others
        responsible for your justice, when it comes from
        within, more terrible and intimate than a faceless
        judge and cold contrivance of execution.
May you live, I say, as long as it takes for you to own
        what you did, may the coldness turn to grief,
        and the grief call out for judgment.
May the judge in you be just, and the fearful mystery
        of your penance unfold within.

Willow, NY, April 1996

THE SHAKER

Clicking seed pods in Amazon canopy
crickling knees of a cricket in dry grass
urgency in the rhythm coming
across great bodies of water
to seek you out

Lifeline of the singer,
            the story-teller
      the dancer in flight
who lands on the moveable surface
of grumbling stones

Arroyo of rattlers
who have eaten the water
and spit out insistent noontime heat
insects that harry the sleeper
aphrodisiac dreams

O traveler
close to the bones across evening prairies
shaman's apprentice, salute
to the threshold between
the worlds.

Soledad Prison, CA, January 1998

ABUSE

for Kim Wozencraft

I sit hunched over in a train,
reading the story of a woman
locked up for killing
her man

But I don't know that
right away. She doesn't let it out,
not even to herself
She maintains
she makes sure all the sounds
she makes are capable
She survives.

I sit hunched over in the train
reading how he hit her
& hit her & hit her
until passivity buried her voice
until she backed into a corner
and would not speak
until all the blood ever shed
seemed like her fault

I sit hunched over in the train
and see no matter how painful
it will be
she will find her voice again,
she will.

New York City, January 1994

CALIFORNIA

California sky—no snow, no freezing rain
       no hunched shoulders worried
about the
long
icy driveway. Or so it seems.
       The slate gray ridge line west of Soledad
fogged in now like Tibetan Plateau
       with majestic Annapurnas hidden
on the left side of the valley, behind clouds.
       Wild white baby yak might be gobbling
rosehips from his side of the bushes.
       But that's
not it. Not as simple as that.
       The real sky has a population of
       seagulls flapping and wheeling
in wild abandon over miles
and miles and miles of razor wire.

Soledad Prison, CA. January 1998

WHICH SIDE ARE YOU ON?

Where does my anger come from
            at the laziness, the prosaic?
How many times will you enter a room
            and leave it vacant: in and out,
in and out, visiting a temple of possibility
            and never leave a gift on the altar?

Come down to the river of your own soul, we are
            excavating
here, the yellow helmets you see are so many
suns on the horizon, going down and coming up
in no particular time sequence or order.
            When one flower opens, Kabir says,
                        ordinarily
dozens open. I'm digressing.

Every time you visit yourself without
            respect, you lose. Without love,
Also.
Read the coins you've thrown down into the dirt,
            they spell *integrity.* You recall those
early moments in
your young life when you sang. And we were
            witnesses—if not then, now. We can
                        see you
outside the ordinary, grab onto a miracle and
understand it was no more you than the
            wind.

Oh, so that's it, finally.
No more you or me than that mountain
    there. And no mountain either.

    Which side are you on?

Eastern C.F., Napanoch, NY,
June 6, 1996

THE JOB

Out on the fire escape with the vinegar
and the rags, looking in at her
setting the yellow formica table,
the plates and the forks,
Daddy's black watch cap by the telephone
he's lying down in the back room
until supper.

Stuffed cabbages, my favorite
she's filling the bowl
the windows are squeaking, no streaks
no lint in the corners
I love this job, watching the kerosene stove
kitchen warmth, and my place
at the table between Irene and Willy

And out here also, looking at the night
close down on November backyards
the light inside growing, clothes on the washline
flapping in the intermittent wind
That's enough, Janina, they are clean enough
Get your brother now. Come and eat.

Eastern C.F., Napanoch, NY, March 1997

246

In This Place

Like the ruffled skirt of a cancan dancer
   or an Aymara woman in the marketplace
       the frilly mushroom at the foot of the oak,
an acorn in its petticoats

Mist rising from the valley, a silver sun,
   sustained drone of cicadas and the wet
       gurgling frogs put me to sleep
I dream of doors opening in the rock behind me

And perhaps these are different paths to you
   An ant steals a piece of the popcorn
       I have left as an offering
A yellow jacket noses down and flies off with a chunk

They make me laugh.
   Who am I to delineate your appearance?
       I love you, whatever door is the one
I always have and I always will.

There goes the ant with an even bigger piece.

North Lake, NY, September 1996

GRANDMA

Maybe I shouldn't attribute human feelings
to a forest, maybe it doesn't cry
when its single trees are culled and cut and dragged out
maybe if the doctors said your grandma had gangrene
in her hands, you would let them chop off
her fingers, one after one
her ring finger she hated to part with
she howled as her thumb and forefinger
hit the ground. She is quiet now, stumps
where fingers were. How will she hold you?

To someone like me, who passed her house
and pulled her berries, and dug her leeks
out of the hillside, and lost myself
in the dappled leaves,
I guess I took her for granted
waving at me sometimes from her porch.
I'll miss those hands.

Flanks of Tremper Mountain, NY,
Valentine's Day, 1998

American Landscape

The field of grasses midsummer high
moving in languid wind beyond the threshold
along with the stags and buzzards gives the lie
to those unnaturally cloistered in the stronghold

Across the American landscape in the night
past darkened houses and empty churches drive
forty miles in any direction, follow the light
to its source inside a razor-wired hive

Old monasteries and inns have been replaced
by a world of prisons, the lights in the distance
without a welcome, the humming machine a waste
land without produce, its workers in a trance

What apparatus is this we've tacitly blessed
that separates two million citizens from the rest?

Eastern C.F., Napanoch, August 1998

249

OUTCAST

I am hunkered down
the curve of my back down to the coccyx
I am hunkered down in the marketplace
meeting, saluting, holding my place
at the wall

there's an etiquette in the choreography
of us coming and going, sharing a moment
sometimes we stand
sometimes we sit, rows and rows of us
without moving

On the edge of action, just at the threshold
is where we lean weighing the possibilities
Out in the sky I speak openly
in a loud voice, without holding
back laughter or the tears of love

Rock me to sleep on the belly
of a black sea, the tide relentless
as it pours across the dike
and the whole village comes to stand
mouths open in the roaring surf

at us, squatting there on the edge.

Eastern C.F., Napanoch, NY, October 1996

For Rabindranath Tagore

a kind of script for F. T.W.

With your little *y*'s, your lower case *t*'s
saying *you* to God as to a friend,
saying oldtimey *thou* to the one who knows you

When I met you in the dusty Paris bookstore
standing on a ladder, holding your book
understand I came fresh from Jerusalem
fresh from the towering Yahweh perspective
where as a woman I was not permitted to dance
in the street for Simhas Torah

And when I tapped a man on the shoulder, one of
the Hassidim forbidden to look any woman
in the eyes, except his wife
when I deliberately interrupted their meditations
on Jaffe Street, saying,
Excuse me, what time is it?

and watched them time and again look away,
understand I was trying to crush those daggers
sticking out of the serpent's head,
I was trying to say,
Look at me, I also love
that one

and the one I love is not far away
the one I love inside me is my friend

251

Revolutionary! What an idea!
Kabir said it, Rumi said it, Mohammed said it,
you said it, Mira Bai said it
Solomon said it in his song

How can actions be separate from prayer?
I write the poems, and sell the books
and with the money buy the flowering bushes
for your garden
where I love you, where I sing to you
Is there separation?

It is all lower caste, all of us outside
the city walls, sitting
not uncomfortably in the dust and camaraderie
without any visible means of support
It is all lower case, all you and i
inside the revolutionary heart.

Willow, NY, July 19, 1996

WELL, YOU NEEDN'T

Wobbly passage down a rickety track
even though you always know
      you may be the
last to divine a direction. There's
      a courage in this, and not a
little grace. Fact is

You and me, we
owe ourselves an
unprotected stance under the sun

Not pushing with the solar plexus,
      insisting on our own terms
even when they march off the bridge
Everywhere we go, this possibility
dogs us: Freedom

No ego driving the boat, no lover in pain
      but a wide circumference
that need not know its name.

Eastern C.F., Napanoch, NY, January 1998

HUNCKE

You mention Ponderosa Pine
and I am catapulted back
way back …
The first time I heard you read that piece
I was sixteen and you had cheekbones
jutting out into the night of cafeterias
42nd Street dives and intellectual cafes

There was a purity of belief
you have always believed in goodness
your voice hovered over the circle of listeners
like a disembodied story teller
the midnight talker, last
of a long line, fascinated
with the curious details

From your Chelsea Hotel room window
where I looked out at the 23rd Street
crowded afternoon, you said,
"Look, our sitting here and talking, you and I,
this is the spirit for me. *This* is God."
and I agreed.
"I knew you would," you said.

You told of the dolls
a parade and series of dolls
left on top of the garbage cans outside
your window on 7th Street, and the one
hanging by the neck above the entrance
just before Louie died, and the voodoo doll

254

you showed me once, with the seeds in her stomach

They pricked anyone who pulled up her dress
"What about her?" I said.
"Did you dump her onto the heap
in the corner of the backyard with the others?"
"No," you said.
"I could never work up
enough disinterest to throw her out."

Like the little details
you brought into the stories
that lit them up and engraved them
on the brain pan,
despite the demand for pedestrian fact
you could never work up
enough disinterest to leave them out.

Eastern C.F., Napanoch, NY, August 8, 1996

ELISE

for Elise Cowen

Thirty-five years after the fact
I read your poem, addressed to Mr. Death
a love song you never showed me

I remember that time, the two of us
on a bus through Queens or Brooklyn
coming back from an all night psychedelic journey
Mescaline, perhaps, I was laughing and laughing
and the laughter was infectious, you also
were laughing, and the other passengers
riding to work, we were suddenly all
giggling in the sunny cold morning

I didn't know then what I have learned since,
that the coded messages from one's own psyche
need not be private, nor decipherable
since then I have learned these songs
from the center of oneself
are also from the center of everyone else
and the God I yearned to grasp I held within
since then I have learned that all love
is a face of that,

that there are no misfits, no stragglers,
no one left out of that effulgence
There's a passage through the white cabbages
you said I said,

256

a cryptic communiqué mailed
from the psyche to the girl who traveled
and the way she envisioned was a way we walk
in the life or out
a pathway back to where we came from

you were so eager to wipe out the traces
to hurl yourself through the plate glass window
believing you needed to smash your way through
the goddess of compassion
who looked out of your eyes at us all,
all your friends, would have, given time,
perhaps turned and witnessed
your own quiet and demanding beauty

It was something you had to do.
Now thirty-five years later, you are the young one
the twenty-nine year old, angry at herself
who could not believe she knew
the way home.

Willow, New York, Halloween 1996

ALLEN

Raking the yard I realize
you are everywhere now
I went down to the river
broke a coconut for you, threw it
into the white water spring flood
so like you
sun behind the tree, the flesh of the coconut
bobbing in the water
like a skull in the breeze

I remember that poem you saw us
walking away from the boat
with our skulls, white coconut meat
Your infinite grace in connecting people, I never
saw you miss somebody's name, making
introductions, leaning in with thumbnail
sketch of personal accomplishments,
a vast networking consciousness
in you, all the writers

and reporters, all the teachers and
musicians—you were the hub, the axis
A sixteen year old kid in a parking lot
stops me last night, he loves your work
and the men in the prison workshop ask for
your book, that mugging poem they especially
like, no one these days untouched
by your unswerving politics
your heart compassion

Mark Twain, born with Halley's comet
left on Halley's return
Hale-Bopp enters, brightest
emissary we will ever see from the stuff
of creation
and fittingly you take it out
like the F Train from Second Avenue
Don't be sorry, you said, speaking
of your death,
I've been waiting all my life for this

I remember the gallon jug of death vine
ayahuasca you brought from the Amazon
you were the first to speak about
the radiance I believed in
A timeliness in your actions, running
for the news, creating another
possibility: bare knuckled
warrior poetics
Pack a small bag & hit the ground running
rushing like a river with a coconut rolling
bobbing in the water

My last dream of you, you were thin
you were sitting on the floor
Peter brought me in to see you
you were singing to somebody's guitar
You ran out to the corner for news
and returned
to a room filling up with love,
of people past and people present
Hey Allen, everywhere now!

Willow, NY, April 6, 1997

259

The Rose

Rumi says choose the wine
where no fear lives.

I placed a red rose in a hole I dug
behind the outhouse, in the sun.

The man said plant it by a wall
to keep it warm when the cold comes.

I said if it's supposed to thrive, it will—
on a slope, in clay, in wavering pine shadow.

When fear entered it was I who called it,
married to a pleasure I might lose.

Attached to yesterday I died there,
rocking on my haunches in the debris.

In the saints, Rumi says, is the wine to drink.
They are pouring it right now over your head.

Step outside the noise of surrender,
only unbound love can hold the rose.

Eastern C.F., Napanoch NY, September 1998

Mr. Ray

for Ray Bremser

What's to say, Ray?
We have to stop meeting like this
What about our fortieth reunion?
It would have been next year
since the Seven Arts, since the Village
Bonnie sitting on the floor
you hatchet faced skinny blues walker
keeping high above the cloud cover,
all that smoke through all those years

Your apartment on the Lower East Side
late mornings, was that 1968?
we listened to Coltrane, talked about scoring,
you and Bonnie my prototypes of hip compassion.
That bare light bulb in Hoboken slum
before or after your going on the run
and the time of your absences
jail after jail, parole violations
Bonnie always waiting your return

What's to say? We go into the corner
of choice when we die
We know the way.

Your unlikely bucolic arrival in Rosendale
the loudest drunk at The Sturbridge Lion,
at my reading, your voice in the dark called for

Exhortation, my poem for you,
and I opened the book after fifteen years,
and closed it again
I could not read it, it was too far behind me.
How much we take for granted—
that there always will be friends who need us,
that there always will be voices in the dark
requesting poems.

Out on a pilgrimage, spring 1988,
going everywhere I knew love would be present,
from Cherry Valley I arrived at your door
in Utica, second floor rooms over after-hours
liquor store, wrong side of the tracks
I read you my talismanic letting go of love poem,
you in the one good chair like Buddha, center of
the empty room, backdrop of bottles
                    stacked like soldiers
and overflowing ashtrays, the big dictionary
like a personal friend beside the radiator

"Sis toe lee, dee ass toe lee," you said,
correcting my "sis-tole. Die as stole."
"Naw," I said. "It'll throw the rhythm off."
"See for yourself," you said,
hatchet faced Buddha in cadaverous chair,
and you were right.

"Are *you* happy, Ray?"
You nod at the ashtray, the army of bottles,
"I have emphysema, cirrhosis of the liver,
I'm trying to cut back..." your gravelly
New Jersey voice, "but I'm content."

262

Last week setting out for western New York
I stop for gas, the woman at the counter
in her everyday talk speaks in loose cheek
hollow vowel sound
Pulling away, I play it back in my head
Where have I heard that sound before?

It's you, sblibbity-bopping word machinator
spilling 'em out like marbles
from your hollow mouth sound, your thorax axe

What to say, Mr. Ray,
what to say?
We've been through this before.

Goodbye, Ray.

Naples, NY, November 1998

BLUEBERRY PANCAKES

for Erin Black, Brenda Frazer, Eila Kokkinen

Bonnie, Eila, Erin, Janine.
I can see us in the dark wet streets
of New York City, 1959, 1960, 1961
kicking over the traces
of Union City, Washington, Chicago
young hot women heading toward a dawn
eager for the romantic life
where everything would turn out fine

Now Erin wears a hat
she holds an armful of blooming catnip
Bonnie in her dress and work boots looks like
a woman in the 1930's, her fine boned face
from a dustbowl American landscape
she has brought a ripe melon
Eila those days with manuscripts, in the company
of admired men, brings blueberries

all of us grown into selves
eccentric to the world
Keeping a pig in your basement?
Painting for years in rural America
without a car? Living in shady woods with deer
and raccoons for company?
Holing up in the office without answering
the door, the e-mail, postal mail, or phone?
And here we are.

264

What of the others?
Inez, Ayesha, Barbara, Michelle
we weren't many, we knew each other:
women in a world predominantly male
who leapt off the edge with the same intent
that has brought us here, the same earnestness.

We walk around and take each other's picture
We tape the talk. We are reaching back
like sisters, call it love, to the time
we were that becomes us

touching as we pass
each other,
four
ladies in a garden.

Willow, NY, July 1998

S.H.U.

So they say he was a long thin man,
        nevertheless they said they could not see him
        through the window. He had simply vanished
        like an idea in a blank mind

        They said they had to run around
        a corner, unlock some gates, and chains,
        it took a while, by the time they found him
He had hung himself. Imagine a body in mid-air
        Nothing to hang from, nothing to hang with
        No rope no tie no hangman's noose, the goose
        is cooked, the man is gone, imagine that.
        In solitary confinement,
under continual surveillance, he disappeared.

        He was a menace, they said. Had escaped once,
        might try again. Had thrown feces at them.
        His teacher said he was a very bright man.
        Crafty and dangerous, they said. Yipping and barking
        like Mohicans heard through European ears,
        they busted in, all six of them,
        covered in riot gear, masks and helmets, flailing
        batons, they dragged him out, and just as
        they said, he was dead.

        A brush fire flitting across their faces, all the way
        out to the gate, that smile of shame.

Upstate New York, February 1999

The Draft

Walking out or into a prison for the fiftieth or hundredth time
to encounter by chance a "draft,"
the bringing in of prisoners to their new abode,
to watch the men shuffle in in shackles
ankles in chains wrists in chains
ordinary men, their dignity crumpled about
their feet like regulation greens on the floor
of the crapper, where do you put your eyes?

How, like Pablo Neruda, who came holding out
his hands in front of him, filthy from the blood
of the mines, can you take no part in the crime?
Called "on the draft," a routine procedure,
as though naming it would efface the squalor
a euphemism like "on the way to the showers"
at Auschwitz, "she's on relief detail for the troops,"
how do you witness? Where do you put your eyes?

In World War I, World War II
men drafted to defend their country
are pulled in now to bolster an industry
building on their shackles at the bottom of the pile
two million strong. Lamp shades, anyone?
And to see it weekly, regularly, to come upon it
fresh at the gate, or the central cage,

or the bench on the guardroom floor,
do you engage the man who does not want
to be seen with rage in your eyes? With compassion?
Do you look somewhere else in the drab

267

environment for relief? Do you ignore
the chains the civilization you belong to
put on his hands, his feet? Do you bow your head
in shame? Do you ask for forgiveness?

Careful no trace of it reaches your face, you
double over with the sucker punch
you are on your hands and knees in the sewer
plowing through defilement
Uniformed men corraling raw material into clumps
are workers in the world, like you
engaged in the transport of people in chains
as a day job, how does that feel?

If this were an isolated instance
you could tell the story to a shocked world
rocked in its innate decency to demand redress
but it is common

The cruelty has grown from random acts
to a root cause the size of a grapefruit
a tumor in the heart of a people
and try as you will there is no way to avoid it
or engage in gallows humor and forget it,
there is nowhere you can turn and not see it,
the guilt of complicity falls on the shoulders
of all who will not speak, who avert our eyes.

Willow, NY, March 12, 1999

268

Comet

for Cecil Boatswain & The Harvest Moon Collective

Over hills and fields
over roads and ridge lines
over forests rushing headlong
fixed in place,
a longhaired traveler
from the beginning of time
a dirty snowball flung from the schoolyard
of wheeling planets, fire and ice

As though I'd been given a glimpse
through a door, chance of a lifetime
and time and again a flashlight
blocked my vision through the keyhole,
as though I were looking for a history
older than dirt
older than animals slope-shouldered
crossing the road

and I listened for it
with seven people in a prison classroom
all of us leaning in at news of freedom
a letter from somebody's home,
a letter with wings
and something took flight
in each of us, like a bell struck deep
reverberating outward

From lightning bugs rearranging space
to aurora borealis red
over August fields, this alertness
to light, like a smudge on the hill
To catch it driving, with peripheral vision
the tail growing daily, hugging the horizon
eyes blinded again and again by headlights
in rearview mirror, and still intent

on finding it
there
like the muezzin call to prayer
somewhere out there over the desert
that yearning
for what it comes from, for where it sings.

Willow, NY, March 27, 1997

270

BIRD MOTHER OF CÁGLIARI

for Anne Waldman

Ancient mother
    enshrined on shelves
        from Cúcurru'e Mari in Sardegna

a row of little mothers from Cúcurru S'árriu
    Early Bronze Age to Medium
        Bronze Age (1,600 BC), Nuraghic Civilization

Bird Woman carved in white marble
    with wide square shoulders
        and sightless beak,

Do you think
    by surrounding ourselves with images
        and artifacts of the old way
we could be thrown back,
    jarred, taken by surprise to our ancient
        self and its singing heart?

Our introspection down sinewy tunnels
    the cavernous hold of your arms and knees
        your dark night a starry
maternal church, with nesty cognizance
    of a physical world and its clutch of eggs
        each more wonderful than the next

Could we walk back to that garden
   and recognize your obsidian blades
      your round chamber house
your hand in front of
   mons veneris
      as you turn to the right?

Could we nod and duck into that kingdom
   protected, procreative
      without the wars of division?

Could we find you, consolation,
   as we take up on our shoulders the work
      that admits no separation?

Could we find you
   smiling at the door
      as you welcome us home?

Cágliari, Sardegna, July 1999

Printed April 2000 in Santa Barbara &
Ann Arbor for the Black Sparrow Press by
Mackintosh Typography & Edwards Brothers Inc.
Text set in Giovanni Book by Words Worth.
Design by Barbara Martin.
This first edition is published in paper wrappers;
there are 200 hardcover trade copies;
100 hardcover copies have been numbered &
signed by the author; & 22 copies lettered A–V
with an original artwork by Janine Pommy Vega
have been handbound in boards by
Earle Gray & are signed by the author.

PHOTO: Max Schwartz

JANINE POMMY VEGA went from Union City, New Jersey to New York City at age sixteen in search of the Beat Generation whose books she'd been reading. She met Gregory Corso, and through him the other writers. After graduating high school she moved permanently to New York. In the fall of 1962 she left America with Fernando Vega, and traveled with him for three years through Israel and Europe. After his death in 1965 she returned to America and finished her first book *Poems to Fernando*, which was published by City Lights Books in 1968. In San Francisco she spent time with the Diggers, Hell's Angels, and North Beach writers, and lost four successive manuscripts for her second book.

In 1971 she left for South America, and lived in Peru, Colombia, and Bolivia for the next four years. During her stay on the Island of the Sun in Lake Titicaca in Bolivia, she finished *Journal of a Hermit* and *Morning Passage*. She returned to New York in 1975 and began teaching poetry to English-speaking and bilingual children in public schools, and to prisoners in the New York State Prison System. Her travels during the Eighties and Nineties formed the basis for *Drunk on a Glacier, Talking to Flies; Threading the Maze; Red Bracelets; Tracking the Serpent; Island of the Sun* and *Mad Dogs of Trieste*. She is presently the director of Incisions/ Arts, an organization that brings writers into prisons. A member of PEN American Center's Prison Writing Committee, she is the co-author with Hettie Jones of *Words over Walls*, a handbook on starting a writing workshop in prison. She has received grants from New York State Council on the Arts, S.O.S., and the Puffin Foundation. She performs her work with and without music around the world.